MW01128475

PRAISE FOR RISE ABOVE

Prepare yourself to enjoy life's lessons of faith, generosity, and perseverance. Jerad will share how to continue moving forward through the journey of life.

—Roger Staubach
Two-time Super Bowl Champion, VI and XII, Super
Bowl MVP VI, NFL Man of the Year 1978

The lens in which your eye's see the world determines your opportunities. That is what *Rise Above* is about. Even through the struggles he endured, Jerad saw many opportunities with his positive mindset, faith, determination, and perseverance. As a former teammate of his, I recommend reading this book. It is inspiring that through hard work and dedication you can reach the highest mountains and hilltops.

—Emmanuel Sanders
Super Bowl Champion L

Humility and a servants heart are what come to mind when I think of Jerad Romo. Sharing, caring, and encouraging are on full display. Jerad's decision to write this book and share his life experiences will be a blessing to whoever reads it.

—Thomas Morstead
Punter for the New York Jets, Super Bowl Champion XLIV, Author of *The Middle School Rules of Thomas Morstead*

Rise Above reads as a reflective narrative describing the surprises that life presents after it has kicked you around a bit. With a spirit of gratitude, Jerad recounts his transition from athlete to businessman and from boy to man. There's relatability in overcoming challenges and the growth that comes from learning to see the bigger picture. This book is a reminder that if you want something bad enough, you will always find a way.

—Kelvin Beachum, Jr.
Offensive Tackle, Arizona Cardinals and 2018 and 2021 Walter Payton Man of the Year Nominee

As Jerad's college coach I recommend his book. I watched him firsthand live through faith, perseverance, and generosity. Anyone who is looking for encouragement and enlightened experiences will find it here. I'm extremely proud to have been able to watch Jerad carry this from the football field to his daily life and career. I think without a doubt his story can help others.

—Coach Phil Bennett
Head Football Coach SMU, 2002-2007

The story that Jerad tells is about his journey of the American Dream. Life has its difficult turns, but if a person builds their journey on faith, family, and hard work, they can achieve their goals. Jerad has demonstrated through his life that if a person works hard and is not afraid to step out of their comfort zone, they can continue to strive forward with a successful and happy life.

—Coach Steve Denman
Head football coach, Tehachapi High School (retired)

RISE
ABOVE

STORIES AND LESSONS
FROM THE MOUNTAINS
TO THE HILLTOP

JERAD ROMO

MEDIA.COM

Rise Above

Published by
Illumify Media Global
www.IllumifyMedia.com
"Let's bring your book to life!"

Library of Congress Control Number: 2023923324

Paperback ISBN: 978-1-959099-64-2

Cover design by Debbie Lewis

Printed in the United States of America

DEDICATION

To my family

The world can be a tough place and will present trials and tribulations. Family sticks together through it all. I hope this book provides a respite from daily life and can be used as fuel to positively change lives. May you hold your head high and continue marching forward.

CONTENTS

ACKNOWLEDGMENTS

The saying "It takes a village" couldn't be more accurate. I have so many people to thank, and I love you all. While I can't mention everyone by name, please know that I appreciate you!

I thank my parents, who have always been there for me. You love endlessly and never let me stray too far from the path. I love you very much and appreciate how you raised me.

To my sisters who are my biggest cheerleaders. You are always in my corner, listening, laughing, and smiling. Thank you for always loving me.

Teachers and coaches, you are doing the Lord's work. You mold children's lives' daily. Thank you for the impact that you had on me. I wasn't always a willing student. Thank you for pushing me.

Principal Jim Hollen, you kept a watchful eye over me for six years, from middle school through high school. Thank you for gently nudging me to think about the next steps of my future.

Coach Denman, thank you for pushing me to play quarterback. Putting me at the quarterback position taught me valuable life lessons and forced me to mature into a man. Becoming a quarterback changed my lifestyle decisions and for that, I'm very grateful.

Coach Brent Carder, I can't thank you enough for redirecting me toward playing football at Antelope Valley College after a rough patch of baseball at Bakersfield College. I was at a dead end with my baseball career, and you welcomed me back to football. The opportunities you provided me changed my life. I am eternally grateful and miss our conversations.

Coach Bennett, offering me a scholarship to play football at Southern Methodist University in Dallas, Texas, was the greatest gift I could have ever imagined. The journey was tough, but we ended on a high note with three game victories in a row to complete my senior year. If I could do it again, I wouldn't change a thing. The highs and the lows prepared me for successes that are greater than any dreams I had as a young boy in Tehachapi, California. Thank you for your continued friendship and guidance.

Carl Sewell Jr., thank you for listening to my story at the Dining with Decision-Makers Dinner at Southern Methodist University (SMU). I was incredibly anxious at the event and didn't understand what professional possibilities were available with Sewell Automotive Companies. Our relationship started that night and set me on an unimaginable business trajectory. Thank you for seeing something in me and believing in my potential.

Roger Staubach, your personal and professional example is admirable. I was challenged to find someone as a model for my life who had achieved significant successes and make myself vulnerable to learn from that person. I shot for the stars and persisted for special time with you. Thank you for your friendship and for allowing me to learn from you and your family.

To my wife, Ashley Romo, I've been in love with you ever since I met you. Your smile lights up a room and you exemplify greatness. I knew that if I wanted a life with you, I needed to strive for and accomplish greatness. I work hard for you and our family, every day, and love what we've built. I can't wait for what's to come! I love you!

FOREWORD

There's something special about Division 1 student athletes. To compete at the highest level of amateur athletics, these students develop time management skills, resilience, competitiveness, and respect for leadership. They know when they need to be a member of the team, and they know when they need to lead. These are skills that serve them well throughout their lives. I've had the opportunity to observe these characteristics in the many outstanding student athletes I've met in my years as an administrator in higher education. It makes you wonder what setbacks and successes have fed these strengths.

It was seventeen years ago when former Mustang quarterback, team captain, and MVP Jerad Romo shared his story at one of my favorite SMU Board of Trustees events. Each year, SMU students are invited to apply to be a speaker at the SMU Board of Trustees' annual Dining with Decision-Makers event. Selected students attend the spring Board of Trustees dinner to share their thoughts and interests with a distinguished group of business, civic, and philanthropic leaders. Our trustees enthusiastically look forward to this evening.

When Jerad Romo shared his story with the trustees in spring of 2006, he had been named Mustang offense player of the year and started an SMU football turn-around after a heartbreaking 0-12 season. He led the team to a victory over crosstown rival TCU, handing the Frogs their only loss in an 11-1 season. But until he spoke that evening, who could know of the injuries, disappointments, and homesickness that might have derailed another football player's career? Those of us who heard him speak learned more about the strong family ties, work ethic, and dreams that were—and are—the backbone of Jerad's character.

We knew he had developed the strength of character, leadership skills, toughness, and self-confidence to be a success in whatever field he chose. With the encouragement of friends and family, Jerad chose to share his story in this book, hoping it would be an inspiration to others. I know it has been an inspiration to me.

—R. Gerald Turner, President,
Southern Methodist University

INTRODUCTION

As a little boy in the mountains of Tehachapi, California, I had big dreams of athletic achievement. My ticket to success was a Division 1 athletic scholarship that would give me financial backing and exposure needed to pursue a career in the NFL. Was this far-fetched? Possibly so, but I believed wholeheartedly that I was capable. I wanted to be the person who fans loved and cheered for, so it was time to prepare.

By the end of my senior year in high school, I was MVP of football, basketball, and baseball and our senior class president. Everything was aligning toward my success, but I struggled to catch a break. My big dreams came to a screeching halt when I didn't receive any athletic scholarships for Division 1 schools. *Should I hang up my pads now or attempt to compete at the junior college level?* I wondered.

My first two years of athletics out of high school were brutal. From all the successes in high school to many struggles in college, it was extremely difficult to continue to hold my head high. However, my family never missed a beat believing in my ability. Finally, a couple miracles happened, and I made it to the hilltop to attend Southern Methodist University in Dallas, Texas.

Eventually I did get paid to play sports professionally. This was the dream that I always wanted, but when

I got there, things were different than I expected. It was not what I envisioned when I was a kid. *What should I do now? Were there different plans for me?*

Later, as a business professional, my friend and fellow associate Klint Guerry suggested that I write down my thoughts and lessons learned from conversations, meetings, classes, and books I read. I've cherished the quiet time journaling to reflect on how situations from my past have caused me to pivot, learn, and grow. A handful of these inspirational quotes and lessons that helped me rise above are included in this book.

Additionally, with the help of mentors mentioned in this book, I was inspired and pushed to be the best version of myself. With their guidance, I experienced many special times and events at SMU. These included some athletic accomplishments, earning MVP honors for the football team, and being selected to speak to the Board of Trustees of SMU about my journey from Tehachapi to SMU. My coach told me that if I came to the university, I could help the program achieve extraordinary levels, receive a great education, and have an opportunity to marry a beautiful woman. Each of these dreams came true.

Buckle your seatbelt because this journey has many twists and turns. I hope this book will allow you to envision your journey, lean on those in your inner circle, and take risks. Keep getting up when the world knocks you down.

Like the mustard seed, we are all so small and hope to blossom to the best version of ourselves. May this book encourage you in faith, generosity, and perseverance to change the world.

1

DRESS THE PART— BORROW A SUIT

When I arrived at Southern Methodist University (SMU) in Dallas, Texas, I was one of five quarterbacks playing for the Mustangs. The competition for starting quarterback did not concern me. I knew my leadership skills on the field would play into my battle to the top. My job was to focus on my goal not on my current circumstance. I worked hard to prepare myself for the job at hand. If given the opportunity, I would deliver results as a quarterback leading his team to victory. Little did I know that becoming a starter on the field would open doors for me off the field.

In 2006, I was asked to present a speech to the Board of Trustees of SMU, a group of prestigious businessmen and women in the Dallas community. As a senior, and as the quarterback of the football team, I was asked to explain how attending SMU had positively impacted my life. The event was called Dining with Decision-Makers, and they wanted to hear about my life and the transition from Antelope Valley Junior College in California to SMU in Dallas.

While I was flattered to be invited, I was incredibly intimidated to speak in front of people, especially this group. The Board of Trustees were successful, polished, and affluent, and I didn't even own a suit! What words of wisdom could I offer and how could they relate to me, the young man from Tehachapi, California?

After thinking it over, I decided to decline the offer. I was dating a girl named Ashley at the time and told her that I was invited and that I was going to decline the invitation.

"Do you realize the opportunity in front of you?" she said.

"I already have a job and I want to play in the NFL. I'm not doing it."

"Don't be foolish," she said. "You need to do it."

"I'm not going to do it," I retorted.

"Yes, you are," she commanded.

"Yes, ma'am."

I've learned that when your girlfriend or wife speaks to you with conviction, the best answer is, "Yes, ma'am."

I contacted the organization and told them that I would attend and share my story. Ashley and I started preparing for this event. Over the next few weeks, we put together a speech about my life and journey to SMU, and I practiced the speech out loud in my bedroom. Ashley will tell you that she wrote the speech, but since it was about my life, I guess I can take credit for it.

The night of the event finally arrived. I was as ready as I was going to be. I was proud to be a part of such a special event but felt like a fish out of water, completely out of my comfort zone. I borrowed a suit and tie from my roommate's dad and had him tie it for me since I had never done it before. It was *go* time and I was ready.

Ashley was my date, which really put me at ease. With her in my corner, I could do anything, and I wanted to make her proud.

When we arrived, my anxiety increased as we were assigned to different tables for dinner. The intimate evening began with dinner in the library of a small building on SMU's campus. I was lucky enough to sit by Mrs. Gene Jones, the wife of Jerry Jones, the owner of the Dallas Cowboys. With my burning desire to play football in the NFL, I believed this to be a match made in heaven. As we were enjoying dinner, I looked down at the ground and saw a large diamond earring. I picked it up and then looked at Mrs. Jones. She was missing an earring, so I handed it to her. She was astonished that it had fallen out and was beyond thankful that I recovered it for her. Naively, I just knew that this was going to be my ticket to the Dallas Cowboys. Now, the night was all worth it! I was elated.

Dinner came to an end, and I moved to the head table with three other SMU students who were selected to tell their stories. The time to deliver my speech had come. My heart was racing. I was lightheaded, but I looked out to the audience at Ashley and with confidence, delivered the speech that we had prepared. I shared the following story.

I grew up in Tehachapi, California. The city limits sign shows a population of six thousand people. Twenty-five thousand people live in the surrounding areas. The town has one stop light, one blinking light, four elementary schools, one junior high, and one high school. We finally got a movie theatre when I was in fifth or sixth grade.

When I was thirteen years old my parents taught me that if I wanted something in life, I would have to work for it. I started mowing lawns, making pizzas, bussing tables, pouring concrete, framing houses, and working in the grape and carrot fields. I was not proud of all these odd jobs. I asked my parents why all my friends were able to spend the days playing video games and playing with their friends.

They responded, "Because we are going to teach you that if you want something in life, you will earn it."

In my senior year of high school, I played three sports: football, basketball, and baseball. My school principal, Mr. Hollen, also talked me into being the senior class president. After my senior year I thought that my future was secure. I earned the MVP award for football, basketball, and baseball. I always wanted to play Division 1 football and I knew that this would get me there. Unfortunately, that didn't come true. At the end of high school, I had zero Division 1 offers. I had a lot of decisions to make.

I felt like going to junior college and earning my way to Division 1 was the best route. I moved to Bakersfield, California, with my grandparents and attended Bakersfield College to play baseball. I played the whole fall baseball season and learned quickly that this wasn't going to get me where I wanted to be. I had never quit a sport in my life, *but I decided it was time to quit and transfer to Antelope Valley College to play football.*

In October of 2001, I contacted Coach Brent Carder, and he welcomed me to the Antelope Valley College football team with open arms. I reset my mind and worked hard on my physical fitness to prepare myself to compete in football. My whole freshman year was spent competing in the offseason of baseball followed by the offseason of football.

The football season finally came around, and I was ready to prove myself. The second game of the season was in Santa Barbara, California. In the first half of the game, I broke my collarbone. I hurt my shoulder and stayed in for two more plays because I thought I just had a dead arm. When I came off the field, the trainer stuck his hand under my pads and realized that it was broken. My teammate signaled to my parents that it was broken, and I remember seeing them put their heads into their hands. They couldn't believe it. I stayed with the team for the game and rode the bus home with them. That was a miserable six-plus hours.

When I got in to see the doctor, he told me that I would have to miss the whole season. This meant that I did not compete for two full years after high school. With the help of my parents, family, and friends and a special comeback song from my dad, Steve Winwood's "Back in the High Life," I would get myself back up and prepared to play again.

Junior college taught me the discipline of hard work. I worked in the carrot fields with migrant workers for sixty hours per week, 6 a.m. to 4 p.m. Monday through Saturday for minimum wage. After work I would lift weights and play 7 on 7 at Antelope Valley College. During football season I worked at Home Depot starting at 5:00 a.m. watering the garden. As soon as the store opened, I collected shopping carts until about 10:00 a.m. Then I would go to class. After class I would lift weights and then go to football practice and then night school.

After my collarbone healed, I was back for another season. I played a game against Robert Johnson, the best junior college quarterback in the country, from Reedley Junior College. Many scouts came to watch him, and I had a good game. This put me on the map. After he was recruited to Texas Tech University, I got exposure to Texas Universities and got a scholarship to SMU.

I drove my manual transmission Toyota Tacoma with manual windows and manual locks across the country. I got to SMU and informed Coach Bennett that before we talked, I needed to get all my belonging out of the bed of my truck. He put his arm around me and informed me that I could leave it in my truck all semester long because nobody at SMU wanted any of my belongings. I knew then that I was in a different place.

I was third or fourth string on the football team. At one point, I called my parents and said that I wanted to go home because I was lonely and homesick. They told me that I needed to stay and let me know that the same things that worked in Tehachapi, California, will work in Dallas, Texas. Stay the course!

Over a two-year period, I earned the starting quarter-back position, captain, and MVP honors for the offense. This is critical because if I didn't earn the starting position, *captain, and MVP honors the Board of Trustees wouldn't have wanted to hear from me. Performance is your ticket to admission to anything you want in your life.*

After the dinner I went over to the table where Ashley was sitting. Mr. and Mrs. Sewell, the owners of Sewell Automotive Companies in Dallas, were sitting next to her. Mr. Sewell was at the event because he was the chair of the Board of Trustees of SMU at that time. He told me that he loved my story about perseverance, overcoming obstacles, and doing things that most people aren't willing to do.

"You will be very successful," he told me. At that point in time, I didn't quite believe it. I didn't own a suit. I didn't know how to tie a tie. And I didn't know how to make the transition to the business world.

He then looked at Ashley and said, "She is driven, attractive, talented, and competitive. She will be very successful as well." He then looked back at me and said, "Son, if you are with her, you must be one heck of a salesman." I took that as a compliment and smiled.

Little did I know that that night would open a door to a career at Sewell Automotive Companies. The story goes that Mr. Sewell really wanted Ashley to work there, but instead he got me by default.

LESSONS TO RISE ABOVE

You have to trust in your ability to learn.
—Sankaran Venkataraman
MasterCard Professor of Business Administration
University of Virginia, Darden School of Business

The way you get better at everything is to start getting better at something.
—Jose Bowen
Educator, Scholar, Musician, Consultant

Each time that you felt you should've said something, you were right.
—Joe Stallard
Chief Human Resources Officer
Sewell Automotive Companies

Whatever it is that you want to succeed at in life, personally or professionally, few skills will serve you better than the ability to take the long view.
—Matthew Kelly
Motivational Speaker and Business Consultant

2

IT STARTS AT HOME

The factors that led to my being invited to speak at the Dining with Decision-Makers event are many. My parents, sisters, and extended family were always steady and supportive of my dreams. I learned at a young age how to think big and work hard. I learned how to cultivate relationships. I was taught to treat people with kindness and respect and to give my best effort and not take anything for granted. I had an open relationship with my parents. We talked candidly about successes and failures and took responsibility when things didn't go our way.

My family was so close knit that it was a difficult decision to leave California and drive to Texas by myself. I was venturing to a new city, with new teammates, without the comforts of home for support. It was a risk, but my family made me believe that attending SMU would provide opportunities beyond what I could understand. I'm grateful for my dad's wisdom and for encouraging me to make the leap and attend college in Texas, far away from home.

My extended family also supported my dreams from a distance with handwritten notes and words of affirmation, regardless of whether things were going well or not.

Grandparents, aunts, uncles, and cousins also made the effort to travel to games to watch me play. Their presence was the greatest gift. I understood the financial sacrifice they were making to come to Dallas and show their support, and I was so proud to show them around SMU's facilities. These trips reminded me of the importance of having a support system and made me cherish time with loved ones.

I can see now how the environment that my parents and grandparents created has impacted all my relationships as an adult. And now that I am a parent, I can incorporate what my family taught me into raising my children.

Jerad Romo with his extended family from California at SMU.

ROOTS

My parents, Karen and Jim Romo, were married in 1978 and are still married today. I was born June 15, 1983, in Santa Maria, California. My mom was raised in Santa Maria and went to Santa Maria High School. My grandparents and many of my aunts, uncles, and cousins live there. When I was about three years old, we moved to Orlando, Florida. My dad worked as a contractor for Martin Marietta Aerospace Company for a couple years before being transferred. At five years old, we moved back to California and eventually settled in Tehachapi, California.

I have two sisters, Karly, who is three years older than me, and Lindsay, who is five years younger than me. We were a hard-working, middle-class family that valued discipline. This was engrained in me from an early age. Our home life was loving and nurturing, yet competitive. My sisters and I were taught to never settle and instead to shoot for the stars. My parents believed there was always room for improvement, and that we could push beyond what seemed reasonable.

As a young boy in Tehachapi, I attended Golden Hills Elementary. We rented a house within walking distance of the elementary school. Our neighborhood was filled with kids our age, and we enjoyed the freedom of outdoor play with our neighbors. I became fast friends with our immediate neighbors, the Schneider boys. Josh Schneider, who was one year older than me, and I spent many hours riding bikes, playing sports, and enjoying the outdoors of the neighborhood. Little did I know then that I would later compete with Josh for positions in high school.

I walked to and from school with my mom, which was a lot of fun. One day, my mom was late meeting me at school to walk home. Even though I was only in kindergarten, I knew the way home and started walking. Much to my mom's surprise. I made it all the way to the front door on my own. Our town was incredibly safe and allowed me to gain confidence and independence.

Eventually, my family moved to a house on Gold Street where I lived for the rest of my time in Tehachapi. We still attended the same elementary school and were able to ride our bikes to and from school. We also spent a lot of time at Meadowbrook Park. The park was in our neighborhood, and we frequently rode our bikes to our ball games or to watch our friends compete. This was wholesome living, the stereotypical American dream.

Both of my sisters and I had great friendships and played many sports through high school. Karly and Lindsay participated in softball, basketball, volleyball, and swimming. We all played in the band as well. Karly and Lindsay played the flute, and I played the saxophone. The full schedules kept us busy and out of trouble. Since we knew everyone in the neighborhood and at school, we couldn't get away with anything. Parents in town would report back to Mom and Dad if we were ever out of line.

My full schedule would continue through the summers. Playing baseball with my friends was a major highlight of summertime. I played in the Little League

All-Stars for Tehachapi every summer. The DeGeer family, who had only one child, bought a fifteen-passenger van to drive my teammates and me all over the state of California for different baseball tournaments, weekend after weekend. We would crack jokes, play baseball, and share incredible times. It was a strong community and those trips provided hours and hours of bonding and provided me access to youth sports. My parents weren't always able to attend because they were working, so I learned to respect others and be on my best behavior. I also learned how to take care of myself on the road.

In middle school, I expanded my friendships. Tehachapi is a city with four elementary schools, one middle school, and one high school. Eventually, everyone ends up in the same school, so all my friendships carried through the years.

As a sophomore in high school, I made the varsity teams in three sports: football, basketball, and baseball. I was the only sophomore on the football and basketball teams. Dustin McBride, a good friend of mine, was the only other sophomore who competed with me on the baseball team.

Because I was on the same teams as the older kids, my friendships changed and caused me to mature quickly as an athlete. I watched how the older guys were training, working out, and improving. If the upperclassmen were in the weight room or taking extra reps, I wanted to do it too. These relationships engrained in me a strong desire to push for growth and results. I wanted to compete at the top level. I wanted to be in the game. I wanted to win.

VALUE OF A DOLLAR

When I was thirteen, I started mowing lawns. My parents raised me with the understanding that hard work will help you achieve your goals and dreams. I had one customer named Spencer, who my mom met when she was waiting tables at the restaurant. He had a big house out in the hills of the Tehachapi mountains. He hosted weddings in his backyard from time to time and was very particular about how he wanted his lawn cut. He wanted me to mow the lawn twice around the outside with two circles around the edges. On the right side, he wanted me to mow the lawn in one direction and in another direction on the left side. Every time I went to his house to mow his lawn, he would whistle and ask me to stop the mower so he could explain what he wanted me to do. As a teenager, I was irritated with this man, but it taught me great lessons about satisfying a customer's wishes and doing a job exactly right each and every time.

I also mowed a lawn at a business in town. The school bus would drive by this location, and students would see me mowing the lawn. I always felt embarrassed when my friends saw me working. Looking back, it was probably a great example to others about making money and how I spent my free time.

On Sundays, when I was thirteen or fourteen years old, I worked at Branch Office Pizza with my mom. I learned to make pizzas, sandwiches, and salads. This was a great time to learn the value of a dollar and work closely with my mom. Waiting tables is hard work, and again, I learned how to please the customer.

When I was sixteen, my mom responded to an ad for an experienced construction worker. I was not experienced, but my mom believed I could handle the job. She took me straight to Dan Knowles, the hiring manager at Bear Valley, and told him that I would show up and work hard every day. While he was apprehensive, he agreed to hire me for the summer.

On June 15, 1999, I turned sixteen. My mom drove me to the Department of Motor Vehicles to get my license so I could drive myself to work. I passed the test, and from that point forward, I drove myself back and forth from work each day. I learned the importance of accountability and time management. I was in charge of the wheel and now had to get myself to work on time.

That summer, we built Mr. Knowles' personal house from the ground up. I poured the concrete, framed the house, and put the trusses on the new roof. I still drive by this house from time to time and admire our work. I was learning every day but am so thankful for the experience. I learned to trust my coworkers, practice my Spanish, ask questions, and strive for perfection. Mr. Knowles admired my work ethic so much that he let me hire my friend Kris to join me at work for the rest of the summer. We made many memories.

LESSONS TO RISE ABOVE

Go where you are needed the most. Don't worry about the title.

—Joe Stallard
Chief Human Resources Officer
Sewell Automotive Companies

Ability may get you to the top, but it takes character to keep you there.

—John Wooden
Award-Winning American Basketball Coach and Player

You must compete in the part of your business that is the toughest for the competitor to emulate.

—Dr. Hemang Desai
Program Director for the SAP Social Sabbatical
Co-founder at Ray of Hope International Foundation

Ensure that you are worth more than your pay.

—Steve Mulvany
President and Founder, Management Tools, Inc.
Professional Speaker

3

SILVER PLATTER

Competing in sports was my sweet spot. Through athletics I made great connections and friendships and learned a lot about life. I began competitive sports when I was young and continued throughout all my formative years. The struggles and victories have shaped me into the person I am today.

My football career journey and dream of playing in the NFL was filled with many twists and turns, successes and failures. A football game can have many sudden changes. Managing the changes for a victory requires focus, commitment, teamwork, and skill.

In football there is no failure, just lessons learned, a concept that can be applied to other facets of life.

GUT CHECK

Playing football for Tehachapi High School was the highlight of my young adulthood. On Friday evenings, the entire town shut down to watch the Warriors play "mountain football." Due to Tehachapi's elevation of four thousand feet, it was colder and harder to breathe for our opponents. Thirty minutes away from town, the elevation dropped to one hundred feet. Being prepped for the elements gave us a huge home field advantage. As a young boy, I couldn't wait until the day that I was able to play for Coach Denman under the lights, in front of a full crowd.

Coach Denman was an incredible man. He played quarterback for the Warriors in high school and returned as head football coach in 1982. He led a winning tradition and prided himself on creating great men in the classroom and on the field. He was a man who everyone respected. He held his players to a very high standard, focused on the fundamentals of the game, and knew how to win the right way.

When I was growing up, my parents didn't want me to play football due to the physical dangers of playing a contact sport. In sixth grade they finally gave in and allowed me to play. My parents took me to register for the season. At the weigh-in we realized my weight was going to require me to *play up* at the junior level, which meant that I would be playing with mostly seventh and eighth graders. Although I wanted to be tough, I looked up at my dad and told him that I didn't want to play. I'm not sure how that made him feel, but I appreciated that both he and my mom were okay opting out at that time.

In seventh grade, I reconsidered and decided to play. The coach put me in at running back and linebacker. Both positions seemed to be a natural fit for me, and I truly loved playing football with my teammates. There was something special about this game, especially in Tehachapi. We learned as youth football players to run the Wing-T offense. Every program funneling into Tehachapi High School ran this offense so by the time that we played for Coach Denman we had the system down. We weren't the fastest or the biggest in our league, but we worked relentlessly in the weight room, and we knew our assignments. We did things right, carried out our fakes, and pounded our competition every play. We willed ourselves to victory by executing the basics.

When I entered high school in 1997, Coach Denman put me on the junior varsity squad as quarterback instead of running back and linebacker. Being a responsible coach, he had watched me play with his son, Chris, and thought I had potential to be successful as a quarterback. I trusted Coach's judgment even though I was not comfortable playing this position. I was playing a sport that I had only been a part of for two years, with older players who I wanted to fit in with, in a position that I didn't know. This was a significant time of growth for me. Things that are so natural for a quarterback, like taking a snap from the center, were not easy for me. I struggled. I still had to learn the basics.

Our team also had a very talented sophomore quarterback. This was a kid who I grew up with and learned a lot from. When he was in the game as quarterback, I asked Coach if I could play running back, wide receiver, or linebacker. I just wanted to be in the game and help the team. Little by little, I found my way into the starting lineup as quarterback and helped lead the team to an undefeated season. At the end of the year, I got moved up to the varsity team for the playoffs.

My sophomore year was filled with challenges. I played second-string quarterback on the varsity team behind another neighbor of mine, Nick Swihart. I was the only sophomore on the varsity team. I was young but willing to challenge the upperclassmen. Nick and I drove to school together and then competed for the same position on the field. It was challenging for both of us, but through that relationship I learned how to balance friendships and still compete at a high level. I had the skillset but probably wasn't mature enough for the responsibility of leading the team. Like the previous year, I found a way to play running back or linebacker when I was not playing quarterback. I did my best, but the players were now bigger and stronger than me. I just wasn't in my element.

As the year continued, I received tremendous opportunities. The first-string quarterback got injured, and I found myself in the driver's seat. I learned quickly from game experience and made adjustments that led us to victory. Each week, I studied the competition and prepared my mind for Friday night. Our team finished the season 6-5 after a first-round playoff loss to Sierra High School.

Now that I was the first-string quarterback, I began receiving recruitment letters from many Division 1 schools. This added to my confidence as a football player and increased my desire to continue playing football in college and beyond.

My successes continued to snowball my junior year. By then I had played with the seniors for two years and felt comfortable with them. We hit our stride and had many great victories. The season led us to the second round of the playoffs where we met Sierra High School again. At halftime, we went into the locker room confidently tied at 14-14. However, Sierra came out strong and scored twenty-seven unanswered points in the second half giving them a decisive victory. Though disappointing, it was time to go back to the drawing board and start building again for the next year.

During our senior year our team was positioned to have a record-breaking year. The seniors had known each other since elementary school, competed in many sports together, and were ready to make it a special year. A California Interscholastic Federation (CIF) Championship was our sole goal for the season.

We knew our offense and defense inside and out, worked hard in the weight room, and loved each other. This committed group had a special bond you see in the movies. We knew how to play together, and we knew how to win. Coach Denman pushed us to the point of perfection and didn't allow us to compromise our vision.

My senior season began with a momentous 56-6 victory over a very competitive team from Bishop. After the game, Coach reminded us that this was only one game, and we had a lot of football left to play in the season. Doing something special takes performing consistently day after and day. Back to the drawing board we went to prepare for the coming weeks. After the first six weeks of the season, we had demonstrated our dominance. We were winning by large margins and felt like we couldn't be stopped. However, weeks seven and eight presented some challenges. We had two tough opponents; we prepared thoroughly but ended up losing both games by one point each. We were in a tough spot but as a strong leader, Coach kept pushing us.

He asked, "What were we going to do now? How good do we want to be? How would we finish what we started?"

In week nine, we bounced back with a big victory, setting us up for our next game against our greatest rival, Garces Memorial High School. Tehachapi High School hadn't beaten Garces on their home field since Coach Denman's son, who was now playing on our team, was born. Garces even designated the game as their homecoming, which is typically against any easily defeated opponent. We were irritated and hungry to avenge our past losses. We were focused and ready to do what we did best, which was stick to our plan and play our game. As the dust settled, we came out with a big 34-10 victory. I played the game of my life, running for four touchdowns. Additionally, my dad graduated from Garces High School, so this win was personally sweet. This was a great day for my whole family and a very proud moment. With that win we secured a tie for first place in our conference and were ready for the playoffs.

We had a history with Sierra High School. In 1998, we lost to Sierra in the first round of the playoffs 20-56. In 1999, we lost to Sierra in the second round of the playoffs 14-41. In 2000, our team won the first two games of the playoffs and were set up to face Sierra again in the championship final. Our team knew Sierra inside and out. We'd played them two years in a row. We knew their schemes, we knew their players, and we wanted revenge for our previous losses to them.

The game didn't disappoint. Going into the end of the fourth quarter, we were down 7-14. There were a few minutes left. The game had been a wet, muddy defensive battle. Both teams came ready to play. Both teams were led by great coaches, and it showed.

With thirty seconds left on the clock, we faced a fourth and long situation. I dropped back to pass, saw an open receiver, and let the ball fly. Just as I threw the ball, I was hit in my side. With the wind knocked out of me and the crowd screaming, we came down with the ball. My teammate, Josh Barker, started running toward the endzone and was tackled inside the ten-yard line. Our team had arrived, and we were positioned for the win. With no timeouts and the crowds roaring, I got up off the ground and looked at my coach. He was telling me to spike the ball. I knew what to do.

While trying to catch my breath and get to the line, I got disoriented. Our team lined up, and rather than spiking the ball, I turned and handed it off to my running back, Dustin. Sierra came through the line, tackled him, and laid on him as we watched the clock run out. The final score was 7-14. We lost again. We were the runner-up. *How could this have happened?*

I could make excuses, but I was the leader. I was the quarterback. I missed my assignment. Some lessons in life are harder to learn than others, but this one was heartbreaking.

After the game, my dad came into the locker room, and I just cried. I was inconsolable. That game was devastating. *Could I ever play football again? Was I the leader that I believed that I was? How could I ever face my teammates again?*

It was time for a gut check. After some time passed and with the help of my family and mentors, I learned to get back on the horse and start training again. Win or lose, I learned to hold my head high and live for another play. This was just the beginning of my journey.

FORK IN THE ROAD

Once football season wrapped up, it was time to move my focus to the next sport: baseball. During the baseball playoffs of my senior year, we found ourselves, once again facing Sierra High School. It was a huge game for us. Many athletes in the area played multiple sports, so literally, we were battling against the same players from the previous football season. Sierra had beaten us in the football playoffs of my sophomore, junior, and senior years. Not only that, but Tehachapi High School had never won a baseball CIF championship before, and we thought that this was going to be our year to finally come out on top.

The playoff rivalry game started off with a bang. I was the starting pitcher and was feeling confident. After getting three outs in the field, it was time for us to bat. I came up to the plate in the first inning and hit a homerun. It always felt good to hit a homerun, but this particular at bat was bittersweet. This was going to be our game; this was our time. The game was tight, but we finally came out with a victory. We beat Sierra and put ourselves into the championship game for the district.

The championship game was held at Bakersfield College, thirty minutes away from Tehachapi. They had a beautiful field just a few blocks down the street from where my dad grew up. I was considering playing baseball and football there, so it was going to be extra special. Our opponent was Liberty High School, who we had beaten earlier in the season. They were from Bakersfield, so although this was a neutral field, it was more of a home game for them than for us. But our fans traveled well, and there was lots of energy in the stands.

I started the game on the mound for the Warriors. Several scouts attended the game. Some of the scouts had watched my dad play when he was growing up in Bakersfield. This was a special time. Scoring went back and forth throughout the game. But in the last inning, Derik Easttom, our pitcher, was on the mound. He had perfected his pickoff move from first base, and it came in handy. With one runner on base and two outs, Derik executed his pickoff move to perfection. He threw the ball to Mike Halpin on first base, who caught the runner in a pickle for the final out. We did it! We had finally beaten Sierra in the playoffs and knocked off Liberty for the final game. We won our first championship in Tehachapi High School baseball history. The celebration was incredible and being seniors, competing right down the street from my grandparent's house, in my dad's hometown, made it extra special.

Immediately after the game, I attended a football recruiting event at Bakersfield College. I was on cloud nine from winning the baseball championship and was still in my baseball uniform when I went over to the football field with my family. I was ready for a warm welcome from the coaches, but I didn't receive it. Several other quarterbacks were there, and I felt like I got the least amount of attention out of all of them. I was incredibly discouraged. The sentiment only grew deeper when I heard a coach refer to a quarterback from Canada on the news as *the real deal.* This whole experience really put a damper on my night.

Still remembering how my final game of high school football ended, I never wanted to play football again. I enrolled at Bakersfield College and joined the baseball team.

I played baseball all summer and had a great time. We played many doubleheaders, and I played about half of the time at first base. I was hoping that I could pitch but our team had about fifteen pitchers, and they could all throw significantly harder them me. The chances of me getting on the mound were extremely low, so I committed to playing first base. I learned to embrace my role and do my best to help the team however I could.

The fall semester began, and the baseball season continued. Playing baseball was a lifestyle. We played year-round and practiced constantly. We were on the field practicing for three to four hours a day and were also enrolled in a class called the History of Baseball, which was an extension of practice on Monday nights. I gained deep friendships, lived with my grandparents, and was having a great experience as a freshman in college.

After playing every other game throughout the summer and fall, our coaches informed us that in the upcoming game we would find out where we officially stood on the roster. The rotations would no longer exist and the roster would basically be set since the true season was about to start.

The first game came and went, and I did not play at all. I was ready to play the second game and warmed up as if it were happening. When I came to the dugout to see the lineup, I wasn't on it. This shocked me, but I was more surprised when I saw the starting first baseman was one of our teammates who hadn't played first base the entire season. As the game continued, two more first baseman who hadn't played all season were put into the game before me. By this point I was pissed and totally checked out.

After the game was over, the coach came up to me and asked, "What's wrong with you?"

I gave him an irritated response, and he let me know my attitude was bad. He told me I didn't care about the team. I walked over to the shed and broke down. I'd never faced rejection before. I'd always been a leader, and here I was on the bench with no playing time and in a bad spot with the coach.

When I got home, I called my parents and told them how frustrated I was. They shared the same frustrations and as the conversation went on, it was apparent that playing baseball for Bakersfield probably wasn't going to work out for me. We decided that night that I should call Brent Carder, the football coach at Antelope Valley College (AVC), and explain the situation and see if he was still interested in me playing quarterback for him.

Coach Carder answered the phone, and I was open and honest about what was going on with baseball. He welcomed me back to AVC football with open arms. He told me that they had a football game scheduled for the next evening and that he would love for my family and me to come watch the game. I called my baseball coach and told him that I would not be traveling with the team the next day and needed the weekend to evaluate whether I would continue with baseball. He understood and asked if we could meet on Monday.

The Antelope Valley Football game was amazing. It felt good to be back in the environment and to be wanted as an athlete. Football was something that I loved. I had avoided it only because of the ending of my senior football season and my opportunity to play baseball. It felt great to be reintroduced to one of my favorite games of all time. Coach Carder and the staff couldn't have made my family feel more welcomed.

I decided that evening that I would quit baseball, move out of my grandparent's house, transfer schools, and pursue football again with a fresh perspective. Because I was making the switch in the middle of the year, this meant that I wouldn't be able to compete in baseball or football throughout my freshman year of college. However, I had a clean slate and nine months to hit the weight room to prepare for my first college football season. I missed playing football and was so happy to be back. The future was uncertain, but I was up for the challenge!

FARM WORKER

The summer of 2002 was a year of becoming of man. I had just transferred to Antelope Valley College in January, and I had worked out with the football team the entire off-season. Next on my to-do list was getting a summer job to save money to cover expenses during the football season. I was on my own and needed to secure my finances for the fall. I asked around for leads on companies that were hiring but wasn't finding any prospects. My schedule was demanding, and it was a challenge to find employment that would work around my exercise needs and class schedule. I continued to strike out on jobs that I was interested in, so I started widening the funnel. Time was running out and not having money was not an option.

Finally, with the help of one of my football coaches, Coach Blua, I found a job working in the carrot fields. He informed me that this job would be incredibly challenging, and in many ways tried to talk me out of it. I explained that I needed the money and would do a great job. It was a sixty-hour-per-week job, Monday through

Saturday from 6:00 a.m. to 4:00 p.m. I loved that I was going to get paid for sixty hours per week, but there was one downside. Since the position was farm worker, I wouldn't receive any overtime. I would earn minimum wage for all sixty hours per week. While this wasn't great news, I needed the money to support myself, and I was willing to do whatever it took to be successful.

While many people imagine California with sandy beaches and moderate temperatures year-round, in Lancaster, California, right outside of the Mojave Desert, that is not the case. The summers post a stifling, consistent temperature of 100-plus degrees, and this job was outside work.

When I showed up for work my first day, I met the owner. He and the two managers were the only three English-speaking associates that I would meet all summer. They asked me if I was ready and if I knew what I was getting into.

I said, "Yes sir. Thanks for the opportunity."

They took me out to the field and introduced me to my coworkers. As they met me, they couldn't believe it. Based on appearances, they knew in their hearts that I would not be able to make it through the summer. They hadn't ever seen anybody like me make it more than a week.

As I got set up to begin, the owner left, and I was on my own with my new coworkers. They asked me to hop on a tractor, and we started driving out to our location where we would be working that day. When we arrived, they told me, "*Okay, amigo. Move las pipas seis linas a la derecha.*" (Okay friend, move the pipes six lines to the right.)

Flexible pipes, each about fifteen feet long, provided the irrigation for the carrot fields. Each pipe had an eighteen-inch sprinkler head on one end and a hook on the other end. My job was to grab the sprinkler head, push the pipe forward, twist it to the left to unlock the hook, and move the pipe over six lines to the right. As I looked at the field, I saw more lines than I could set me eyes on and a few hundred yards of pipe ahead of me. I knew it was time to get to work.

My schedule was tough. I started work every morning at six. We worked nonstop until four in the afternoon. I became friends with all the guys. We ate together, sitting on the dirt with our lunch boxes. We found any shade we could for these meals, even if it meant crawling under a trailer for some relief from the sun. Every once in a while, we caught a little nap.

If someone finished moving all their pipes before their coworkers, they could take a break because they couldn't start on the next batch until the team was done. Depending on how they were doing, someone might jump in and help them. Most of the time that was them helping me. I was their equal, and we learned to lean on and rely on each other. As a team, I learned to never leave a man behind. We would start and finish together, as one.

The dedication of my coworkers in the carrot fields was truly astonishing. The balance and efficiencies of their processes were amazing. One coworker knew how to unhook three, fifteen-foot pipes at one time. He would then stand in the middle of the forty-five-foot section and lift all three at once, moving them six lines over. I was in awe. These men sacrificed everything, dripping sweat in one-hundred-plus degrees, working to provide for their families. Many of their families lived in Mexico. My coworkers lived on the property and allowed themselves the bare minimum in order to send almost all their check home every week. I had a great deal of respect for these men who put everything on the line to provide a better life for their loved ones.

Each day when I got off work at 4:00 p.m., I had to drive to Antelope Valley College, which was about twenty minutes away. As an athlete, I still had to lift weights with the team and play 7-on-7 football. I would leave the football field around 7:30 p.m. and finally go home. You would think that I would eat and go to bed, but I was in college. My roommates wanted to hang out and have friends over, so of course I didn't want to miss out. Eventually, I would go to bed, and the 4:45 a.m. wake-up call would come quickly.

If you've ever driven past farm workers on the side of the road, you've seen them covered from head to toe in long sleeve shirts, jeans, and hats. One day, I decided to work on my tan while working in the carrot fields, so I took off my shirt. All my coworkers were staring at me wide-eyed. It was almost like they were laughing at me, as if I was doing something wrong. Eventually, I figured it out. The owner drove by and immediately stopped his truck and started walking straight toward me. He yelled at me, and said that if somebody saw me with my shirt off, he would get fired. Apparently, there are chemicals on the crops that could be bad for your skin, and we were not allowed to be exposed to the pesticides directly. I now realized why my coworkers were laughing at me. It was like when a younger sibling is doing something they shouldn't, and the older siblings egg them on until the parents come. I was the little kid who got busted. I had no idea that I wasn't allowed to work shirtless.

Over time, I became great friends with my fellow associates in the field. We did our best to overcome the language barriers and had many great laughs. There was one gentleman named Roberto who would always say, "*tengo sueno*" (I'm sleepy) in a whiny voice. The guys loved it when I said, "*El nombre de Roberto es no mas Roberto, el nombre de Roberto es tengo sueno*" (Roberto's name is no longer Roberto, his name is now I'm sleepy). They fell on the ground and laughed for what seemed to be minutes. Roberto looked like he wanted to punch me, but thankfully he didn't. That was the moment my coworkers finally accepted me. It was like they had just welcomed me into the locker room as a teammate. They knew that I could do the work, I could speak their language, and I could dish out some jabs. We had a good time. Every day, we got dirty and sweaty and made clean, hard-earned money under the California sun together.

When the summer came to an end, they all told me how proud they were of me. They admitted that nobody thought I would make it through the summer. I defied the odds and was proud of myself as well. I knew that if I could work in the elements and keep up with the demands of my football schedule and social life, then I could do anything. That was the summer I knew I was becoming a man.

BROKEN BONE

After that summer, I began my first collegiate football season and was ready to prove myself to Coach Brent Carder at Antelope Valley College. The second game of the season was in Santa Barbara, California. In the first half of the game, I was tackled and hurt my shoulder. I stayed in for two more plays because I thought I just had a dead arm and could shake it off. I had never experienced a real injury before. When I finally came off the field to be checked by the trainer, we realized that my collarbone was broken. The pain was intense, but the shock of my future was overwhelming. I was devastated. I stayed with the team for the remainder of the game and rode the bus home with them. The drive home was the most miserable six hours of my life, painful physically and emotionally.

The next day, I saw the doctor. He gave me the bad news. I was out for the season. This meant another year of not competing. I was incredibly discouraged but didn't have a choice and began my rehab.

The rehabilitation was grueling and painful, yet I know it made me a stronger person. On top of that, I had to watch my team complete a disappointing 1-9 season. With the help of my parents, family, and friends I would pick myself back up and get prepared to play again.

By the time I returned to the field with the AVC team, I had missed two years of play. I knew my window of opportunity to achieve my childhood dream of playing in the NFL was closing. But in spite of all odds against me, I was eagerly grinning ear to ear as the season started. My passing game had improved, and offensive coordinator, Lon Boyett, told the *Valley Press*: "He's got good judgment and he's real consistent. He's a team leader and he doesn't make a lot of mistakes. That's why we expect big things from him."

The season was up and down for us, but we managed to leave the losing season from the year before behind us. It did not end as we would have liked, but we kept fighting until the end. I did not know then that I would be entering a new chapter in my football career.

Game day picture with my parents, Karen and Jim Romo, after breaking my collar bone.

MIRACULOUS RECRUITMENT

In November 2003 I started communicating with Southern Methodist University (SMU). I was a fifth semester college student in junior college. When I received the call from SMU, I didn't know anything about the university or the mustangs. I had very little knowledge of Dallas or Texas. When I talked to my parents about it, my dad was over the moon. He immediately told me about the Pony Express and the glory days of SMU football that he remembered very well.

I had an opportunity to travel to Dallas to visit SMU over the first weekend of December. I was blown away at the opportunity. Bobby Chase was my assigned roommate for the weekend. Derek Swofford was my host, and everybody welcomed me. The hospitality from each and every person was over the top.

The facilities were state of the art. Compared to Tehachapi, where we had about two thousand fans per game and Antelope Valley College where we had only a few thousand fans, SMU's stadium was a palace. The weight room, locker room, dorm rooms and classrooms were more polished than my previous accommodations.

On that trip to Dallas, I learned that I was recruited by accident. Coach Sawyer was a graduate assistant and was asked to help find a quarterback for the team within a 250-mile radius from North Texas. My highlight tape got in the mix because I played well in a game against Robert Johnson from Reedley Junior College, who was one of the best Junior College quarterbacks in the country.

Coach Sawyer had two stacks of tapes, one with footage from players that they would consider, and another with footage from players they would not consider. Late one night, after midnight, Coach Sawyer decided to watch one more tape before going home. He reached out and grabbed a tape and put it in. It happened to be my tape, and he was impressed with what he saw. My tape was on the discard stack because I was out of the 250-mile radius. Coach liked the film so much that he discussed it with Coach Roark, and the two of them rushed to head coach of SMU, Coach Bennett, to fight for me to get a recruit trip.

My dad joined me on the trip, and we couldn't believe all that SMU had to offer. The beautiful campus, top-notch academics, the SMU network, and an opportunity to play Division 1 football. Even with all of these positives, I wasn't sure if I could see myself moving two states away. Our family was so close, and it was scary to even think about what that would be like.

As the recruiting trip came to an end, I was not presented with a scholarship offer. Coach Bennett said that the staff would talk and contact me over the coming days. If this was going to work out, there would be a quick turnaround because I would need to report to training camp in January, and it was already December.

On the plane back to California, Dad and I evaluated the trip. He could see the opportunities that SMU had to offer much more clearly than I could and said, "If you receive an offer to attend college here, you need to go."

I was offered a full scholarship to play football at SMU the following week. What an amazing feeling this was! I was the only player out of nineteen who was recruited from out of state. SMU was coming off some losing seasons, so it was a huge opportunity to make a difference for this team. I knew it was the best program I could get into, and I felt the team was on the rise.

The following days after receiving my scholarship offer were action packed. We started conversing with the admissions office about transferring my credits to SMU. I wasn't concerned because I accrued seventy-seven academic hours in junior college and needed only sixty to graduate. SMU evaluated my transcript and declined thirty-six of the seventy-seven hours. This left me with forty-one accepted hours, and I needed forty-eight to transfer as a junior.

I immediately petitioned SMU to reconsider twelve hours; they accepted six. I was thankful for the six hours, but I still had a problem. To be eligible to transfer to SMU, I needed forty-eight hours, and I was still one hour short. To make matters worse, I had blown off an astronomy class that I was currently taking, which was part of the forty-seven hours. I had mentally checked out because I already had the sixty hours needed to graduate. My lack of effort was catching up with me, and now I really needed to pass this class to move forward with my future at SMU.

I went to talk to my astronomy professor about the opportunity at SMU. "That sounds great," he said, "but the only way you will be able to go is if you get a ninety-two or above on the final. I will not make any exceptions." As I left his office, I felt sick to my stomach. The highest grade that I had received in the class that semester was a sixty-one. This challenge seemed impossible.

My roommate and good friend, Bob, and I decided to step up to the challenge. We made flashcards, studied the book, and made practice tests. We crammed for three days straight and literally spent every waking hour learning the material. I had to score a ninety-two or above on that final!

In the meantime, SMU needed my official transcript by Monday at the latest—no exceptions. I was pushing tight deadlines on all fronts. I sent the transcript earlier in the week and continued to check the tracking number every day to confirm that it was delivered.

The day of the final finally arrived, which was a Thursday of that week. If I passed the test with a ninety-two or above, I would pass the class and be eligible to transfer to SMU. I had my entire apartment packed in my truck. If I passed, I would return to my apartment and leave that day to drive to Texas by myself. I had to be there by Monday night to begin one final class at a junior college in Dallas to receive my last credit hours. With so many unknowns, I was an emotional wreck. SMU was the ticket to my NFL dream. I walked into the classroom at nine in the morning and took the test to the best of my ability. I felt good but was still uneasy. While my family was celebrating the move to SMU, I was still holding back my happiness because deep down I knew that I might have to unpack my truck and stay in California.

The professor told me that if I came back to his classroom at three in the afternoon, he would have my grade. I would soon learn my fate. In the meantime, SMU said they never received my transcript. I checked with FedEx and the registrar's office, but it was nowhere to be found. I put this worry on hold for the moment and decided to check on my grade.

The walk from the door to my professor's desk seemed infinite. At his desk I stood there frozen with anticipation as he looked me in the eye and said, "Your grade is not high enough." Immediately, tears filled my eyes. I turned around and started walking to the door, wondering what I would tell my family? "Jerad," he called out, "actually you got a 96! You are going to SMU!"

I couldn't believe it. I was overcome with emotion. I felt happy and angry at the same time. How could he taunt me like that? This was one of the biggest moments in my life! I let out a sigh of relief and realized that all my hard work paid off.

Now it was time to figure out my next hurdle, the transcript. I needed to have it delivered to SMU in Dallas by Monday, and I needed to leave California that evening. If it was returned to Antelope Valley College, I wouldn't have it for Monday and wouldn't be allowed to attend SMU.

That's when I realized my big mistake. I had misaddressed the envelope to SMU's registrar's office. I wrote "Ownvy Drive" rather than "Ownby Drive" and it was going to be returned to AVC. I went to AVC's registrar's office and expressed the urgency in the matter. They looked everywhere and couldn't find it. Nobody knew what to do at that point. The registrar's office was about to close for the weekend, and I needed to get to Texas. I needed the transcript to make it to SMU. I called SMU and asked if there could be any exceptions on the arrival of the transcript and they replied with a strong no.

With nowhere else to go, I called Coach Blua for help again. He was off for the day but took my call and said he would come to the school immediately. We were at a loss for direction. The school had closed for the weekend, I needed to leave, and nobody knew where in the office the returned transcripts were located. All that we knew was that FedEx said that it was returned. My transcript had to be in there somewhere!

Coach Blua found an AVC associate willing to open the registrar's office for one final search. All the employees were gone, but we had a feeling that it was in the office. Lo and behold, when we entered the office, the returned envelope with my transcripts was right on top of a pile of mail.

Coach Blua looked at me and gave me a big hug. He said, "Jerad, you are going to SMU! Guard this transcript with your life and start driving to Texas!"

I started my journey that day and slept with the transcript overnight to ensure that it made it safely on the twenty-hour drive to Texas. It was a long, lonely drive. I was leaving my family and traveling to a different city where I knew no one. Through many tears, and another junior college class later, I was finally a SMU Mustang! Little did I know that this new town and new school would provide an opportunity that would change my life in ways greater than I could ever imagine.

Jerad with his Toyota Tacoma truck that he drove from California to Texas.

IRON SKILLET

The competition for SMU starting quarterback was stiff when I arrived in the fall of 2004. Tony Eckert, Chris Phillips, and I were battling for the starting job. I performed well whenever I was in the game. On my fourth possession for SMU against Oklahoma State I ran for fifty-nine-yard touchdown, the only Mustang touchdown of the game. The team suffered a major loss (59-7), but the touchdown proved my versatility as a nimble quarterback who could carry the ball downfield as well as connect with the right receiver and earned me more playing time in subsequent games. It was a personal highlight.

In November 2004, our team defeated San Jose State University (36-13) to break a fifteen-game losing streak, the second longest losing streak at the time. Tony Eckert was starting as quarterback. Late in the second quarter, I was put in the game for a trick play and caught a touchdown pass thrown from wide receiver Matt Rushbrook. In the fourth quarter, as quarterback, I connected with Chris Foster on a pass that he took for thirty-two yards into the end zone.

After that game Coach Phil Bennett told the press, "People asked me has the losing streak been a monkey on your back? And I tell them it's been a five hundred-pound gorilla. I'm relieved." Coach also stated that the starting quarterback position was still open, but he was thinking of starting me in the next game because of my mobility. This was a hopeful point in my football career. I had worked hard, demonstrated what I could do, and all of my goals were starting to fall into place.

On September 10, 2005, one of my childhood dreams came true. I had an opportunity to start my first game of Division 1 college football at quarterback. The stage couldn't have been set any better for my debut. It was the battle for the Iron Skillet, the rivalry between SMU and TCU Horned Frogs of Texas Christian University, who were ranked 22 in the nation. We were coming off a close loss to Baylor at home with a final score of 28-23. TCU had just beaten number 7 Oklahoma on the road 17-10.

Ashley, whose brother was also on the team, was in stadium, and my family and friends were watching the game in California on TV. I was beyond focused. With a few minutes to go before game time, my emotions took over. I called the team to the middle of the locker room and gave the speech of my life. It wasn't scripted; it came straight from my heart!

"We are all here today because we want to leave a legacy for SMU. We all had opportunities to go to other schools, but we decided to come to Dallas. We came here to win. And today that is what we will do. Ford Stadium is our house. We've all shed blood, sweat, and tears on this field, and tonight we will defend our home turf."

I looked each player in the eyes as I spoke, and I knew that they believed. It was time to go to the battlefield.

The game picked up quickly with many hard hits and much aggression, but we were not going to back down. This was a title fight, the battle for the Iron Skillet, and the best team was going to be left standing in the end. TCU's athletes were fast and athletic, but we were sticking with them. DeMyron Martin was our freshman running back and was getting some of his first minutes of college football. When I handed him the ball, he ran downfield aggressively and leaned forward for a few extra yards on every play. This allowed us to keep the Horned Frogs on their toes. Handing off the ball, running bubble routes after faking the run, and putting me on the edge gave us multiple offensive options.

Right before halftime, we were up 7-3 and driving the ball toward the SMU student section in the end zone.

Coach Burns, our offensive coordinator, dialed up a play that we knew would give us a chance for a touchdown. If we could execute this play the way we had practiced it, we would be up 14-3 going into halftime. The ball was snapped, and I faked it to DeMyron Martin. I rolled out strong to my left with a run/pass option and sold the fake. I then pulled up and threw the ball to the far end zone to DeMyron who had snuck around the side after carrying out the fake. The TCU defender played it perfectly. I felt like the ball was in the air forever. As the ball started coming down, the crowd was going crazy. DeMyron caught the ball, was tackled by the defender, and came down with the catch in the end zone. It was his second touchdown of the game, and we were now up 14-3! I was so excited. Jumping up and down, I bumped chests with Chris Foster, our wide receiver. This is exactly how we practiced. Our confidence and our hard work were finally paying off.

We went to the locker room on a high. We were dominating the game on both sides of the ball. The half-time speech from Coach Bennett was pretty direct. We were motivated to finish the game and do something special for our team in our home stadium. SMU hadn't beaten a top-25 team since 1986, and we wanted this victory so badly we could taste it!

We came out of the locker room with fire in our hearts. The crowd was giving us the support we needed. There was something magical in the air. At the second half kickoff, we were ready to set the tone, but TCU ran the kickoff all the way back for a touchdown. We could feel the energy drain from the stadium immediately. It was now 14-10, and we had our backs against the wall.

We remained confident even with all odds against us. Every play was critical. Our best weapon was to keep the TCU defense on their toes, and that is what we did. We repeatedly called zone reads and bubble routes with run/pass options. As long as I made the right reads and held on to the ball, there was no way they could stop us.

Right before the third quarter I ran the ball up the middle of the field. I saw daylight and had one player to beat, then an open field. The linebacker had fallen on his back, so all I had to do was jump over him. If I got past him, I could run for a touchdown. At the last moment, he reached up and grabbed my foot, sending me tumbling to the ground. I landed on the back of my neck and shoulders. Right when I hit the ground, a TCU safety hit me with the top of his helmet in my exposed kidneys and pinned me against the ground. The impact was so hard that my body was literally frozen. I couldn't move, and my lungs were paralyzed. Every other time I had the wind knocked out of me I could at least moan to try to get some air, but this time I was stuck. My body wouldn't move, and I couldn't breathe. My coach ran out and was livid. I could hear what was going on around me, but my mind was in a fog. All the while, the safety who hit me spoke some choice words, letting me know that I'd better stay down. Finally, I was able to moan, roll around, and catch my breath. After a few minutes on the field, I was able to gather my composure. I walked off the field on my own accord and looked up at the clock. There was less than one minute left in the third quarter, and we were still winning.

Having a victory over a team like TCU was my childhood dream. I was in tremendous pain, but there was no way I was going to take myself out of the game. I stayed out for two plays and told my coach that I was okay. Even if I was not okay, I was going back in the game. This was our game. This was my time!

The fourth quarter was a battle. I was hurt, but I was going to do what my team needed. Every time I came off the field my back would tighten up. I needed to do everything I could to stay loose, stay warm, and prevent my back from locking up. Throwing the ball hurt, getting hit hurt, but losing this game would hurt even more. We were going to finish what we started. With about ten minutes to go, we scored another touchdown and were now up by eleven points. Our defense was on fire and held TCU to zero points for the rest of the game. The last four series ended with a fumble recovery, two interceptions, and a stop on fourth and seven. The game finally ended with our offense in victory formation, and me taking a knee to win the game. It was awesome!

The aftermath was amazing. We did it! We beat a top 25 team, I won my first game as starting quarterback for SMU, and SMU football was back on the map. The students and fans rushed the field, and we held the Iron Skillet trophy in our hands. It was incredible!

All the heartache leading up to that point was worth it; growing up working odd jobs, attending two colleges prior to SMU, and experiencing the emotional hurdles of getting admitted to SMU. That game made all those challenges completely worth it. The young boy from Tehachapi, California, had his dream come true in true storybook fashion. It couldn't have been more picture-perfect.

Jerad holding the Iron Skillet trophy for beating TCU in 2005.

After winning the Iron Skillet, our team struggled. We were beaten solidly by the Aggies at Kyle Field in College Station, Texas. The game started with me throwing a sixty-yard touchdown pass to go up 6-0. Unfortunately, the Aggies responded with force and ended up with a stifling 8-66 victory. After Texas A&M, we lost to Tulane at home and then experienced a painful overtime loss to Marshall on the road. After these games, we were in a must-win game situation against the University of Alabama at Birmingham.

BEWILDERMENT IN BIRMINGHAM

One of the most magical evenings of my life took place at the University of Alabama at Birmingham (UAB). The game came down to the fourth quarter with only the last seconds left on the clock, and it was up to me to make the pass of a lifetime to win the game. Steve Lansdale, Pony Fans Writer, said it was one of the most memorable games ever for SMU. Here's basically how I described it in the Pony Fans message board in 2009:

It wasn't very fun talking with our coaches on the sideline after getting the ball back with twenty-three seconds left on the clock because we had been winning most of the game. We hadn't won a game on the road in fourteen games, it was UAB's homecoming, and our entire team was lacking confidence. At this moment, the wind was out of our sail. We were the away team, we were frustrated with our circumstance, and had no timeouts left.

For our first play back on the field, I underthrew the ball to wide receiver Bobby Chase. He came back to the ball because he was heavily defended and caught it an inch off the ground. The referees stopped regular play to review the catch, which gave us a three- or four-minute time-out. During that time, we were able to get organized, which was instrumental in the outcome. Coach Burns, our offensive coordinator, planned ahead and called the next couple of plays, but the environment was still chaotic.

Our sole plan was to get a first down. The clock would stop when the side referees had to move the chains. I would then look to my coach on the sideline between downs to reinforce his play calls. The pressure was building, and it was time to leave it all on the field.

First, I threw a quick swing route to running back, DeMyron Martin. He ran an out-route for three yards and stepped just across the fifty-yard line and out of bounds. On that play, the referees called a sideline warning on UAB, which gave us another minute to reset. During that break Coach Burns said to get in position and execute; we had time.

For the second to last play, their defenders were playing fifteen yards off of our receivers. I threw it to Rey Pellerin on the sideline. I put it on his numbers, and he ran about five more yards and stepped out of bounds at the thirty-one yard line. We had just enough time for one final play.

In the final huddle with my teammates, I said, "Here we go. Let's see what we can do."

Bobby Chase was saying, "'Hey, give me the ball. I'll be open!"

With three seconds left on the clock, we lined up with two receivers on each side for our final attempt to score a touchdown to win the game. Bobby was on the far left side. We were lined up on the far right hash, so Bobby had the wide side of the field available. I knew if I could hurl it *into the end zone, Bobby, who was six foot four inches and determined, would somehow catch it.*

I snapped the ball and launched a hail mary in Bobby's direction. The UAB defensive back was in the back of the end zone, coming forward towards Bobby. The two players collided with the ball at the same time, and had a one-on-one match-up. Bobby jumped and grabbed it. The defender had his hand on the ball, trying to rip it from his grip, but Bobby wasn't going to let it go. Chris Foster, my teammate who was running the seam route, jumped five feet off the ground in celebration when he saw Bobby come down with the ball. It was beautiful!

The whole team rushed the field to celebrate! I was in shock. I remember seeing Bobby go up for the ball, and I thought, oh my God, I think he caught it! And then everyone was running on the field, so I knew we were successful.

I remember thinking about not throwing the ball out of bounds or throwing it short. I had a five-yard by five-yard target to give my team a chance. And it happened! The review time-out of Bobby's first catch really won the game. In hindsight, if UAB had just let it go, we would have been scrambling. By reviewing the play, we were able to come off the field and regroup.

Then we saw head Coach Phil Bennett going nuts. He was not happy, and we were wondering what was going on. The officials were telling him the game's not over. Get your guys off the field. You've got to at least attempt the extra point. At that point, we were up by one point, but theoretically they could block a kick and run it back to win the game. So we had to get back on the line, and I just had to take the snap and take a knee to claim our victory.

The locker room after the game was unbelievable. The victory at UAB and the night after the 2005 win over TCU are the two most memorable times in my football career.

The TCU game was awesome, but we got to down it a few times to end the game. So it wasn't as much of a shock. The UAB win happened in an instant, and the neat part was that it was experienced just with our team and a few loyal fans. We had a few hundred fans travel to the game and everyone was waiting for us at the bus. Bobby's dad bear-hugged me so hard I felt like I broke my ribcage. I was like, you're a little stronger than you think! He just wouldn't let me go, everyone was elated. On the flight home everyone—the players and the coaches—were going nuts. Everyone's phones were ringing off the hook.

Back in Tehachapi, California, my parents connected their computer to their big-screen TV to watch the game. Two buddies from high school came over to watch with my parents. Before the game, they were doing a SMU prayer in a little circle, saying "we believe!", while holding a SMU flag. When I actually threw the game-winning touchdown, my two buddies and my dad grabbed the SMU flag and ran around the street with it.

To this day, my friends and acquaintances all remember that pass, and they remember the TCU game in 2005. When I think about my career at SMU, those are the games that stick out because those are the games we really came together as a team and won. Those were the times we didn't give up. That group was pretty special.

My sports career up to that point had taken many twists and turns with many highs and lows. The unbelievable win against UAB was the pinnacle moment for me and my fellow Mustang teammates. Years later, I still remember the entire experience like it was yesterday. It still gives me goosebumps.

LESSONS TO RISE ABOVE

Practice like you have never won. Race like you have never lost.

—Allyson Felix
Track and Field Olympic Champion

First do what is necessary. Then do what is possible, and before long find yourself doing the impossible.

—St. Francis of Assisi
Italian Catholic Friar
Founder of The Franciscans

Do your job.

—Bill Belichick
Head Coach and General Manager,
New England Patriots

Pressure is a privilege.

—Doc Rivers
NBA Basketball Player and Coach
ESPN Analyst

It's human nature to be average, to just get by. Champions are very special.

Nick Saban
Head Football Coach, University of Alabama

4

PAID TO PLAY

From the time that I was a little kid, I dreamed of competing in the NFL. Chasing this dream included endless afternoons playing in the front yard against my neighbor, Nick Swihart, and competing as if it were the last play of the Super Bowl. We would play catch, practice punting and blocking punts, and kicking extra points. All the while, we pretended we were our favorite football stars with the game on the line. We watched ESPN coverage of the games, wore team gear, and emulated the top NFL players. I hoped and dreamed that I would be playing on Sunday one day.

When I got a scholarship to SMU, I was one step closer to my dream. I knew that if I continued to compete at a high level, I would get the exposure I needed to earn myself a spot in the NFL. As my senior year at SMU came to an end, our season came up just shy of where we wanted to be. If we had beaten Tulsa, we would've been in the conference championship, a bowl game, and received national exposure. Unfortunately, we lost that game and none of that happened. We came up short, losing by a touchdown. With three games to go, our season was basically over. Our record was 2-6 and we were ineligible to compete in a bowl game. But the seniors on our team played with so much heart until the end. With three games to go, we battled and beat Rice, then Houston, and then the University of Texas at El Paso (UTEP), ending the season at 5-6 to provide a significant building block for the teams to come.

I found out soon after completing my senior season that if I would have dropped below twelve hours of classes when I quit baseball in junior college and transferred to SMU, I would have had another year of eligibility at SMU. Due to NCAA rules, athletes are eligible to participate for ten semesters once they start full time classes, which is enrolling in twelve credit hours. In junior college, I played baseball my first year but then broke my collarbone during my second year. I only competed in one football season in junior college and two football seasons at SMU. As a freshman, I thought that finishing my first semester of college with eighteen credit hours was the right thing to do, but in hindsight, it started my eligibility clock and cost me a year on the football field.

You can't always control the events in your life, but you can control how you respond.

With news that my SMU career was ending, I was ready to start my next chapter, training for the pros, but I also still needed to graduate.

Since my scholarship ended in May and I still needed twenty-one hours to graduate, my last semester was stressful. In order to finish on time within my scholarship constraints, I needed to take eighteen hours in the spring and one three- hour, three-week class in May in Taos,

New Mexico. When I tried to register for my classes, the computer system wouldn't let me add the sixth class. I reached out to my counselor; she said I would have to get permission from the dean. The dean told me eighteen hours was too heavy a course load for a student athlete. I left his office very disappointed, but I persisted. I knew my abilities and I needed to graduate.

After searching for other options, I scheduled another meeting with the dean. This was my only option to graduate on time and I needed to convince him to give me a chance. Reluctantly, the dean allowed me to register for the eighteen-hour course load.

After the meeting the dean said, "I can't wait until this doesn't work out, and I will tell you that I told you so." That really irritated me and gave me even more fuel to prove him wrong and show the world that student athletes are resilient.

While continuing my studies, I started working out relentlessly. I was running, throwing, and lifting weights in any spare time that I had. I was getting bigger, faster, and stronger and worked my way up to 230 pounds. I also got a job on campus in the economics department and had an internship at the Gardner Group, a local financial planning company. Between the two jobs, I was working thirty-five to forty hours a week on top of preparing for my pro day at SMU and hitting the books aggressively each day. At the end of the semester, I earned a 3.5 GPA and an apology from the dean. I was now ready for the next steps in my football career.

SMU's pro day was a workout scheduled on campus to showcase athletes' abilities and talents to NFL scouts. This included weightlifting, running, and throwing drills. Scouts from Green Bay, Indianapolis, Cleveland, Houston, and Dallas were there, and I did well. My chances of getting drafted were slim, but it was an exciting process, nonetheless, and I was offered a select workout with the Dallas Cowboys at Valley Ranch, their practice facility at the time. I couldn't believe it. I went to the meeting rooms, tested, got measured, and received Cowboys gear. They gave out shirts, hats, shorts, cleats, and a workout bag. We stretched with the strength coach outside on the practice fields and moved into their indoor facility for the workout. We threw passes and ran drills. Eventually Jerry Jones and Bill Parcells came out to watch us. It was like a kid's dream come true. I was so excited and would've given anything to make the squad.

After the workout, I was invited to play in the twelfth annual National All-Stars Bowl that included college players from all over the southern states who were ready to showcase their talents. Because of these two special events I felt even better about my dreams coming true. *Just stay the course and things will happen!*

The NFL draft was a few weeks later. Although I really didn't think I would get drafted, I watched the event for two days straight. I was waiting and hoping they would call my name and that my phone would ring. The draft came and went, and I never got an offer. Now what?

Henry Sroka, the Dallas Cowboys Scout, gave me some direct feedback. "There are nets in life that catch people in recruiting: you are six foot four and above, you run a 4.4 or below, you broke every record in NCAA football, you play for a legendary coach, or you play for one of the largest conferences in NCAA. Unfortunately, Jerad, you are in none of those nets. For a guy like you to make it, you will need to play in a minor league for five or six years to prove that you are durable and can perform at the necessary level."

After hearing this feedback, I was ready to go down the path. I planned to play five years and prove to the world that I could compete at the highest level. NFL Europe had just shut down and I didn't have any connections to Canada, so the Arena Football League was my next best option. Through relationships with the Cowboys, I connected with the local arena team, the Dallas Desperados, and practiced with their team for six weeks. Since the season didn't start until February, I worked during the day and practiced at night. I truly enjoyed it. Past and current NFL players were present, and I had a great time playing 7 on 7 and associating with these players.

As the season approached, I had a tough conversation with the coach. He informed me that they already had two veteran quarterbacks on the roster and that I could be on the practice squad, but if I wanted exposure, this wouldn't be the best decision. He recommended that I look elsewhere to join a team where I could play right away to get some exposure. I took his advice and stayed focused on my goal. Now it was time to look for another team.

Through Coach Burns, SMU's offensive coordinator, I got a chance to work out with the Columbus Destroyers. I flew to Columbus, Ohio, and had a great, action-packed workout with the team. Unfortunately, I found myself in a very similar place. The team had veteran quarterbacks and did not have a spot for me.

I returned to Dallas a little disappointed. *How am I going to make this happen?* I thought. *Maybe I should give up.* I wondered if I was good enough. I was pursuing all options, but my path wasn't clear. I had another conversation with Henry Sroka about playing for his brother in the World League in Italy. I wasn't ready to let this journey come to an end, so I kept pressing toward any opening that would allow me to keep playing football. Then I spoke with Donald Hollas about playing in the Indoor Football League in Katy, Texas.

After all the dust settled, I earned a spot on the Oklahoma City Yard Dawgz Arena Football Team. While it wasn't my dream job, I was happy to finally receive an offer to play on a professional team. I was so excited about this opportunity but faced some very tough decisions. In order to pursue my dream, I would have to quit my job and move away from Ashley. She was aware of my dreams and desires to play football but was a little apprehensive about this commitment. She had a great job in Dallas, and we had been together for two and a half years. It was very hard to see what the future might look like along this path. Like the advice I was given earlier, this would take five to six years if everything went extremely well. Although the dream was fuzzy at best, I had to do it for me. I packed my truck like I did a few years earlier and moved to Oklahoma City.

I joined the Yard Dawgz and met some incredible people. In my first week in Oklahoma, I met one of my best friends and Yard Dawgz teammate Kenny Williams. He needed help finding the apartment offices, so I showed him the way. We started talking about life and ended up fishing for the rest of the day. We laughed, shared stories about life, love, and football and created a brotherhood that is still flourishing today. He was my family in Oklahoma City, and we kept each other focused and accountable, and out of trouble.

We settled into our new routine: football practices and workouts in the morning and traveling to games with the team on weekends. Everything was great socially and athletically but not so much financially. The salary for athletes in this indoor league was minimal. We earned $250 a game if we won, less taxes, and only $200 if we lost, less taxes. This wasn't going to cover my bills, so I had to find another job to make ends meet.

Due to my new workout and game schedule, finding a job was a challenge. The hours I was available for work were specific and I needed help fast. I worked every relationship that I had from financial planning companies to UPS to Academy Sports and Outdoors, but I couldn't find anybody who would hire me. Finally, I came across a sign at Macaroni Grill, an Italian restaurant, that said they were hiring. I knew how to wait tables and take care of people from my childhood in Tehachapi, so I interviewed for the job. After moving through the process, they hired me. I was happy to finally have a job, but this would mean that I wouldn't get to come home on a bye weekend or off days to see Ashley. But I didn't have a choice. I had financial obligations, and I had to take what I could get.

As time went on, my relationship with Ashley became a challenge. She was busy at her job and doing well socially in Dallas. I was busy too, but not doing so well. I was working all the time trying to make ends meet. I had a college degree but was underemployed and out of money, and feeling down and defeated. I was following my dream, but my dream wasn't looking like I envisioned it when I was a kid. We would travel by bus to most of our away games. One of our games was over six hundred miles away. We left at ten at night so we wouldn't have to pay for a hotel for two nights. Our team funds were low, so we stayed in hotels that weren't very nice, and our travel arrangements were well below average compared to my years at SMU.

Pressure was finally coming to a head. What was I doing with my life? After one of our games, our team bus stopped at a liquor store. The bus rides home consisted of drinking, music, cards, and dice, and I didn't want to partake. I remember sitting on the bus contemplating what my next steps should be. *How could I do this for five or six years? What would the future look like for Ashley and me? What were my dreams? Had they changed?*

With all these thoughts circulating in my head I decided it was time to end this dream. I returned to Dallas and talked with Ashley. I told her that I was ready to come home and be done with football. She was still frustrated at me for leaving in the first place and firmly pressed me to get a job and figure out what I wanted to do with my life. I promised her that I would find something stable, but she was pretty hesitant.

Back in Dallas, I reached out to my old connections to find employment and quickly realized how hard it was to find an opportunity doing something that interested me. I had interviews but was quickly rejected two or three times. I heard all the excuses: you have the wrong degree, we don't have any room for you at the moment, our company focus has changed. *Now what? Should I have kept playing football? Did I make the right decision?*

I soon found myself in Coach Bennett's office. I was down and out and needed a break. Coach told me the best way he could help me immediately was to allow me to help coach his summer football camp. I would be paid four hundred dollars for the week and would be given breakfast, lunch, and dinner. I would need to get there at six each morning and wrap up around eight at night. Although it wasn't much money, I needed it, and I needed the meals. I showed up to camp and started coaching on Monday. I loved it. I wondered if I should pursue coaching as a career. I was lost and many thoughts were going through my head.

While at practice on Tuesday, my phone rang. Covered in sweat, I picked up the phone.

"Jerad, this is Carl Sewell. I heard you are back in town and looking for a job. Is that correct? I also heard that you went into the Infiniti store, and they said they didn't have a spot for you. Is that correct? Jerad, I met you a year ago at Dining with Decision-Makers. I told you that I wanted you to work with us, and when I say something like that, I mean it. I know the Infiniti store doesn't have a spot for you, but the Lexus store does. So long as you go through the process and things work out, I would like for you to start in sales at our Lexus dealership."

I was floored at the opportunity. *Was this the break I needed to put some stability back in my life?*

The next call came from Jerry Griffin, the general manager of Sewell Lexus in Dallas. I was still on the football field in the summer heat, and Mr. Griffin told me that I needed to come into Sewell Lexus for an interview immediately. I explained to him that I was outside in the heat and didn't have any proper clothes for an interview. He firmly stated that I needed to come in today, dressed as I was, and I complied. I showed up at Sewell Lexus Dallas in sweaty athletic clothes and with hat hair, at his insistence. I visited office after office, interviewing with many managers and was overwhelmed with the class of the associates and polish of the dealership. Although I was embarrassed about my appearance, I guess I interviewed well. I was offered a job in sales and began my career on June 18, 2007.

How quickly our fortunes in life can change. One minute I was coaching a football camp on a hot Texas football field, making only four hundred dollars a week plus meals, and the next minute I was vying for an opportunity in a lucrative position with an amazing company,

Sewell Automotive Companies. All the struggle, heartache, and hard work of so many years had finally paid off. All the disappointment and frustrations of not achieving my childhood dream of playing in NFL dissipated as I embraced my new direction in life.

My journey as a professional businessman was just beginning. The NFL chapter was now closed, and my eyes were on the prize, Ashley. In March 2008 we got engaged and were married in January 2009.

Ashley and Jerad Romo entering their wedding reception to the tune of the SMU Fight Song.

This new chapter of my life exceeded all my dreams of being an NFL quarterback. My career at Sewell taught me how to embrace public speaking; polish my manners; work with, train, and lead groups of people; and be relentless with customer service. My life with Ashley got me involved in our church and our community and centered all of our focus on creating the best versions of ourselves in our three children.

The road getting to this point was rocky and sometimes led to dead ends, but the journey strengthened me and grew me into the person I am today. Dealing with all the ups and downs made me resilient. The journey was tough but beautiful, and I wouldn't change a thing.

SWAPPING SUITS

Attending the Dining with Decision-Makers dinner clearly impacted my life. If I had not stretched out of my comfort zone and taken the opportunity to speak at that event, I might never have met Carl Sewell and made the business connection. Without this relationship, I likely would have never been given the opportunity to work for Sewell Automotive Companies. Sewell gave me stable employment, which allowed me to grow up as a man and pursue my relationship with Ashley, and the rest is history.

Mr. Sewell has provided an exceptional work environment that has allowed me to enhance my skills as a leader, public speaker, and service provider. The Sewell organization's commitment to excellent customer service is world renown. And as an athlete, I have been trained to deal with any challenges that arise. I have learned to shift with changing situations, circumstances, and career roles. Nothing is sure except change itself. Pivoting with circumstance, striving for greatness, and performing with excellence in every work endeavor are my focus now.

Athletics and business have many parallels. Athletes must work hard and be disciplined as they prepare to compete. Likewise, businesspeople must work hard and be disciplined to prosper at their work. An athlete or businessman may not feel like working on a particular day, but they show up and step up for the betterment of the team. The skills I learned as a quarterback and an athlete transferred to my business life in more ways than one.

The quarterback of the team has responsibilities of leading the team. The quarterback sets the tone for running sprints and preparing for the season during the off-season when it would be easy to take a break. This includes watching films, working out, eating properly, and hanging out beyond the football field. During the season, the quarterback leads meetings with players and coaches before games to make sure that everyone is prepared and focused for the battle ahead. During the game, as the leader, they must know everybody's assignment. When the defense lines up in a way that would stop the play, the quarterback must make changes and call audibles (verbal instructions) to make adjustments. Each of these skills has made me a stronger businessman. Just as when I was the quarterback of the team, at the store I continue to motivate our associates to work together toward a group goal. Also, as a leader, I've learned to work through conflicts and disagreements and to inspire learning from our mistakes. Through all these skills learned on the football field and practiced in business, I'm able to keep the eye on the prize of constant improvement.

BUILDING BLOCKS

Ashley's grandfather gave me advice when we were driving around town in Fort Smith, Arkansas, one afternoon. He said, "Do you want to know how to be successful in business? You *do* what you *say* you are going to do." It sounds simple, but it's a profound statement. When you tell someone that you're going to do something, you do it.

Cultivating great relationships is about being present, focused on the other person, creating great experiences, and following through on your commitments. Relationships require communication. In the absence of communication people will make assumptions, and those assumptions will become their reality. When you communicate frequently, the relationship grows. When people know that you are truly looking to help them and serve them, not sell them something, they continue to come back, and they tell their friends. As you get more repeat and referral customers, your business naturally grows by maintaining the relationships that you've built. Communication and doing what you say you are going to do are the fundamental building blocks of any business.

Growing up in a close family and in a small town where everyone knew each other taught me the importance of relationships. This certainly helped me on the football field leading a team as well as working at Sewell Lexus.

LESSONS TO RISE ABOVE

The best things in life are not meant to be sped through.
—Carl Sewell, Jr.
President and CEO,
Sewell Automotive Companies

When you create value for others, you will receive value in return. It is the law of the universe.
—Frank Hanna
CEO Hanna Capital, LLC

You must correct mistakes even when you win. Do it right.
—Nick Saban
Head Football Coach, University of Alabama

Your present circumstances don't determine where you go; they merely determine where you start.
—Nido Qubein
Businessman and Motivational Speaker

We are a learning organization. That's what makes us special.
—Carl Sewell, III
Co-President of Operations,
Sewell Automotive Companies

Don't complain about problems; have fun solving them.
—Danny Meyer
New York City Restaurateur
Founder & Executive Chairman of the Union Square
Hospitality Group

5

FOLLOW THE YELLOW BRICK ROAD

The term *mentor* comes from the Homer's epic poem the Odyssey. Mentor was the friend Odysseus entrusted with the education of Odysseus' son Telemachus. In English the term means someone who imparts wisdom to and shares knowledge with a less-experienced colleague. I am forever grateful for my relationships with several mentors who guided me through the peaks and valleys of my youth. From my dad, who guided me as a young kid, to the principal of my middle school, who steered me toward positive relationships, to the football coaches who developed me as a player, I am humbly grateful. Without these relationships, and had I not heeded their guidance, I'm sure I would have veered from the path and lost my way.

EYE ON THE PRIZE

Great mentors and coaches, always push you to be the best that you can be. They help you understand that "good enough" never is and that leadership is performance.

They hold you to the highest standard, allowing you to be the example for the entire team whether that's in sports or in business.

I have received guidance from great coaches and mentors throughout my life. When I wanted to experiment with different friendships in middle school, Jim Hollen, the principal, was always right there to get me back on track. I'm so thankful that he had a vested interest in my future. He was present and took the time and energy to get to know me. He was my middle school principal for two years and then transferred to Tehachapi High School and continued as my high school principal for four more years.

Jerad in cap and gown with principal Jim Hollen

Although we connected over sports, Mr. Hollen helped me be the best version of myself. As a senior, Mr. Hollen convinced me to run for senior class president.

He suggested that I work on my resume to become a more well-rounded student athlete. He also asked me to help our senior class by participating on the executive committee of the student council. Even though I was very uncomfortable and out of my comfort zone, I complied and was elected class president. I grew tremendously through the leadership experience in student council. I now get the pleasure of planning and implementing our high school class reunions that have proven to be extremely enjoyable for my classmates and me.

ON AND OFF THE FIELD

Playing football definitely shaped my discipline and drive. I was fortunate to be coached by some great men who not only helped my game but molded me into the person I am today.

Whenever I had a bad attitude or did not set a good example, my coaches were strong enough to call me out and correct my behavior. In one high school football game early in my career, I was so frustrated that I threw my helmet on the ground. Coach Denman immediately got in my face and told me that kind of behavior would keep me from ever playing football for him again. It was a sobering conversation, and I never threw my helmet again. That lesson taught me how to be a leader for the team and reminded me that people are always watching me.

Without mentors continuously pushing me back on track, I would've drifted off target. Having a great support system of people around me, who knew my family's values, allowed me to continue learning and growing into the best version of myself.

I want to honor these men by sharing their stories.

COACH STEVE DENMAN, TEHACHAPI HIGH SCHOOL

Coach Steve Denman had a stellar coaching career. He retired in 2016, after thirty-five years as the head coach for the Tehachapi High School Warrior football program. During his tenure, his teams won seven CIF Sectional Championships and fifteen league championships. His teams qualified for post-season playoffs thirty-one times. His overall record at Tehachapi High School was 301-118-4 for an overall winning percentage of 72 percent.

Earlier in his life, Steve Denman earned all-league honors as a quarterback for the Warriors in both his junior and senior years, establishing many passing records in the process. He graduated in 1975 and then quarterbacked for the Bakersfield Junior College Renegades and completed his formal education by earning a Bachelor of Science in biology life science from Cal State, Bakersfield.

Coach Steve Denman was influential in my growth. He was a disciplined guy who molded us into great young men. He was not into flashy and fancy drills and activities. Instead, he focused on repetitions of drills done perfectly. Even if the other team knew which plays were coming, we were going to run them so well that it would not matter. He made us believe we could win against any opponent, and we did.

Coach Denman asked me to play quarterback my freshman year on the junior varsity team. I had never played quarterback before. He saw me play with his son, who is one year younger than me, on the youth football team. He told me that I would be a great quarterback, and I would play on the junior varsity to learn the position. These times were difficult. I was the only freshman on the team, and I was competing for the starting quarterback spot against my childhood best friend, Josh Schneider, who was a sophomore. At that point in my football career, I didn't even know how to take a snap from the center. It was challenging to be learning in front of my peers, and in the process, I fumbled many times.

Coach Denman's goal as a coach and teacher was simple: "We try to teach the kids life skills and responsibility. Be responsible. Show up for school. High school academics come before football. Whether being on the field or off the field, be responsible. Those are the things kids will carry on in life."

COACH/ATHLETIC DIRECTOR BRENT CARDER, ANTELOPE VALLEY COLLEGE

Coach Brent Carder played for or coached nine of the Marauders' thirteen conference championships, thirteen of their eighteen bowl games, and was undefeated in playoff games. Native to the Antelope Valley in Lancaster, California, Carder helped mold the area's academic and athletic successes. While most would presume Carder was just a football coach, he was more active in and proud of the off-field accomplishments of his players. He became athletic director in 1975 and in his twenty-eight years in that position, he was deeply committed to the development of the complete person. Coach Carder implemented many measures that helped those participating in the department progress as far as possible personally, academically, and athletically.

Under Carder's direction AVC implemented mandatory drug testing; created an academic support program; and worked with the Marauder Club, the athletic department's booster support group, to ensure athletics were given maximum support while staying well within the guidelines of the governing bodies. Antelope Valley College still boasts more scholar athlete awards than any other community college in California.

In thirty-seven seasons, Carder's teams had a record of 189-185-5, and at the time was the eleventh all-time winningest coach in the nation and fifth all-time in California. Carder himself was named coach of the year in 1974 and 1975 by the California Community Colleges Football Coaches Association and in 1987 by the California Coaches Association.

With all these accolades, I'm thankful he saw something special in me and my abilities on the football field. I quit baseball and was lost, and he welcomed me back to AVC and gave me a fresh start and new perspective. He valued me as a human being and played an enormous part in exposing me to the SMU coaches.

In late 2021, Coach Carder passed away. The Antelope Valley Press named him the sixth most influential sports figure in the Antelope Valley area. In his honor, the campus' stadium was re-named to Brent Carder Marauder Stadium.

Jerad with Coach Brent Carder at an athletic banquet.

COACH PHIL BENNETT, SOUTHERN METHODIST UNIVERSITY

Coach Phil Bennett graduated from Texas A&M University with a degree in education in 1978 and was a second-team All-Southwest Conference defensive end as a senior in 1977. He began his coaching career at Texas A&M in 1979 as a part-time defensive ends coach. He served as assistant coach at seven different colleges. During his first season at Kansas State, in 1999, he was nominated for National Assistant Coach of the

Year. In 2002 he earned the head football coach position at Southern Methodist University (SMU), where he stayed until 2007. After SMU, Coach Bennett coached at Pittsburg, Baylor, Arizona State and North Texas.

Coach Bennett has forty years of experience across the country and has coached in four of the power five conferences. He has coached many outstanding athletes and future NFL players. At SMU he taught my teammates and me to never settle or give up. He challenged every aspect of my game and made me a tougher player mentally. I'm thankful for my scholarship to SMU that allowed me to play under Coach Bennett and compete at the Division 1 level.

Photo at SMU with Karen and Jim Romo and
head coach Phil Bennett

JIM ROMO, MY DAD

My dad attended Garces High School in Bakersfield, California, which is the largest rival of Tehachapi High School, where I attended. He had great athletic successes in high school, winning All League and Most Valuable Player in two sports: baseball and basketball.

After high school, the Boston Reds Sox offered him $10,000 to play class A baseball, but he chose to finish school and play baseball in college instead. He played catcher for California State University, Stanislaus, and helped them win a national championship his freshman year. My dad met my mom at Stanislaus State, where she competed in basketball and volleyball. Eventually my dad transferred to the University of La Verne, and my parents got married. Dad continued playing catcher at La Verne but hurt his throwing arm, which ended his chances to play professionally.

Because of my parents' athletic backgrounds, they were insightful and honest about my abilities. When I was younger, they coached my little league baseball teams and youth basketball teams. Competing in athletics was a family affair, and my successes created many happy memories for our family. I'll never forget my first home run at Tehachapi High School. My dad stood up and yelled in front of everyone, "He is now a man!" That was a very proud moment for me and my parents.

My dad is a storyteller and likes to teach by example. One afternoon, he took me to my high school field to teach me a lesson. During this time, my batting was inconsistent. Dad believed I wasn't recognizing good pitches early enough in the moment. To prove his point, he had me pitch to him. He patiently talked me through our practice until finally I pitched him the ball, and while the ball was mid-air, he yelled, "that's my pitch" and hit the ball over the fence, and over the street. We never measured it, but it appeared that he hit it over four hundred feet. The fact that he could actually do what he was teaching me to do, prompted me to perk up and listen to his coaching. He wanted the best for me, and we both had big dreams for my athletic career.

During my football seasons at SMU, my dad would send emails after each game with his observations about each play. He would always encourage me to demonstrate my abilities to the coaches and to support the team by playing the very best I could in whatever role I was given. He was always very loving and encouraging in his approach. Without the support of my parents, I wouldn't have been strong enough to commit to SMU and stick through the tough times and homesickness. Even though we were states away, I never felt neglected, and they were my backbone pushing me toward my future dreams.

TASK TO GROW

I am blessed that Mr. Sewell saw potential in me, and frankly in Ashley, when I spoke at the Dining with Decision-Makers dinner at SMU. That event was the beginning of a long-standing relationship that moved my career in a positive direction.

Once I joined his organization, Mr. Carl Sewell Jr., the owner of Sewell Automotive Companies, encouraged me and others to *shoot for the stars* when identifying and pursuing the right mentor. He tasked his associates and me to stretch our mentorship goals and learn from people who are the best in their industries. We did this through continuing education classes provided by our corporate office.

Early in his career, Mr. Sewell was mentored by Stanley Marcus, the president of luxury retailer Neiman Marcus. Mr. Sewell shared with me how he gained this friendship, and I planned to duplicate his actions in my attempts to establish a relationship with Roger Staubach, who was most definitely out of reach for me.

Roger Staubach was someone I wanted to emulate in all aspects of life. In order to be more like him, my goal was to spend time with him and learn from him directly. After we met, our relationship grew deeper and deeper, and the lessons I learned were powerful.

I admire who Roger Staubach is, what he stands for, and how he has conducted his life. He married his high school sweetheart and is the father of five children. While he played quarterback for the Dallas Cowboys, he worked in real estate during the offseason to build his professional career. This shows his commitment to the future of his family in case his athletics fell through. Mr. Staubach also served our country in the military. I admire how he carries himself and respects others even though he was extremely successful on the football field and in business.

JUST ONE LUNCH

My journey to get to know Roger Staubach wasn't a slam dunk. I was fortunate enough to cross paths with him many times in Dallas and my persistence eventually bonded us together.

This is how I came to meet and know Roger Staubach.

Over the summer of my junior year in college at SMU, I was working for AXA Advisors. Bob Muskopf, one of my coworkers invited me to play basketball one day at his friend Roger's house. As we were driving to his friend's house to play, he asked me if I knew where we were going.

"Yes, we're going to your friend Roger's house."

"Do you know who Roger is?"

"No."

"It's Roger Staubach's house. I didn't want to tell you because I didn't want that to be the only reason that you wanted to play."

He explained that Roger might be present, and the rule was to only talk to him if he comes outside. If he stays in his garage or inside, then we should leave him alone. He had an outdoor court at his home and different groups of guys would show up for pick up games. I was fortunate enough to be included one afternoon.

When we got to the house, Bob and I played basketball for a while and then Mr. Staubach came outside. We talked to him about playing quarterback, my upcoming college season, and being a leader. It was an incredible conversation that I'll never forget.

A year later, before my senior season, Mr. Staubach was the speaker at a luncheon for the kickoff of the SMU football season. Since I was a captain of the team, I got to meet him with a smaller group. He shared great words of wisdom with our team and helped us prepare mentally for the season ahead.

After graduation, I heard him speak again at an event at the Anatole Hotel in Dallas. I waited around afterward to shake his hand and reintroduce myself. I reminded him that I met him a couple times before, but I'm still not sure that he remembered who I was. Mr. Staubach is invited to attend so many different functions in Dallas because of his notoriety, I was attempting to make a lasting impression.

Years later, when I was in a continuing education class at Sewell, we were asked to consider three goals for the year. My first goal was to slim down to a certain weight to be a more productive associate. Second, I wanted to read ten pages a day, so I could read twelve three hundred-page books a year. Finally, I wanted to establish relationships with three mentors.

After sharing this information and reviewing it within our small group, they encouraged me to find *one* great mentor rather than three average mentors since I didn't have any at the time. They asked me to spend the next month considering who that person would be and report back at our next class. I decided I would pursue Roger Staubach. He was a tremendous quarterback, married his high school sweetheart, served our country, won the Heisman Trophy, was a Super Bowl MVP, and was in the Hall of Fame for both college and the NFL.

Roger and I attended the same church, he was loyal to his family, and was incredibly successful in business. I wanted to be like him.

Mr. Sewell, who took over the company from his father, always told us that we should shoot for the stars when looking for somebody to learn from. He read a University of Texas study that tracked business professionals in the state of Texas who had been inducted into the Texas Business Hall of Fame. They were looking for similarities. Did they all grow up affluent? Did they all go to private school? Were they born in a certain year? Did they attend certain universities? The researchers found that every one of them had a mentor who helped them get from where they were to where they wanted to be in life. The professionals said that without these great mentors they never would have made it. This study is what drove Mr. Sewell to pursue relationships with Stanley Marcus (Neiman Marcus), Erik Johnsson (Texas Instruments and later the mayor of Dallas), and Bob Moore (Bob Moore Automotive). Mr. Sewell shared the story with us many times, and it inspired me to try to find a great mentor for myself.

When I returned to class the next month, my small group asked me who I would like to engage with for a mentorship. I told them that I would like to meet Mr. Staubach, and my class laughed at me. They asked me how I was going to accomplish my goal, and I explained that I wasn't sure but that I would find a way.

Around that time my boss at Sewell, Joe Stallard, asked me to be a mentor for a group called Allies in Service.

This group was intended to help military personnel transition from the military to civilian life. I was never in the military but appreciate what our military personnel do for us. I attended my first meeting of Allies in Service and discovered that Roger Staubach was the founder of the organization. So I got the opportunity to converse with him again. Again, I'm not sure he remembered who I was even after I told him about the other times we met. At that point I decided to reach out to the gentleman who ran the Allies in Service organization to see if he could connect Roger and me on a personal level. I explained that I was being encouraged to find a great mentor and shared with him all the reasons that I admired Mr. Staubach and would love an opportunity to speak with him. He replied that Mr. Staubach was very busy, but he would try to help me. After a few months, he connected me with an associate of Mr. Staubach. I shared with her my hope of a meeting with him, and she said that she would try to help me. After a few months she connected me with another associate of Mr. Staubach. That associate set up a phone call with him. When I finally got on the phone with Mr. Staubach, I explained to him how I had always admired the way he's lived his life and how much I appreciated the personal interactions that we had had with each other. He told me that he was flattered but that he was very busy and wasn't sure that he could commit to a mentorship.

I used the strategy that Mr. Sewell told us he used with Stanley Marcus and asked Mr. Staubach if I could take him to lunch *just one time*. He agreed and we set up a lunch for the next month at Sevy's, a restaurant down the street from his office. At that time, my wife volunteered to be our Neighborhood Association president, which was a pretty thankless job. Ashley managed neighborhood patrols, connected new neighbors, and created a website that included her contact information. Jennifer Staubach Gates, Roger's daughter who was running for city council, was looking for local groups to host meet-and-greet events in the community. Jennifer's campaign manager found our website and reached out to my wife to see if she would host an event for our neighborhood. We decided to host one at our house and I think this decision helped solidify my lunch plans with Roger. It seemed all the stars were aligning, and we were meant to begin a friendship.

As our lunch date approached, I jotted down a page of questions that I would like to discuss. I waited for Roger at the hostess stand and we were guided to a booth in the back corner of the restaurant, where he regularly dines. I was nervous but our conversation flowed comfortably.

After lunch, I went to a nearby parking lot and wrote down everything that I learned during our conversation. I documented the lessons and sent him a handwritten letter thanking him for his time. He told me that as a leader, people won't always like you. However, they will always respect you for having their best interest and the interest of the company in mind. He also shared with me that the way you treat your spouse, the most cherished relationship in the world, is an indication of how you will treat the rest of the world. If you're loving and caring and supportive of her, that is how you will be to the rest of the world. If you are rude, aggressive, and demanding of her, that is how you will be to the rest of the world.

Mr. Staubach also shared the importance treating individuals well no matter their walk of life. It's easy to treat people well who we think will have a positive impact on our life, but how we treat people who cannot help us is really what's important. These three values are a great testimony of someone's true character.

Jerad with his dad, Jim Romo, and Roger Staubach at the Staubach family football game on Thanksgiving.

At work the following day, I walked around the corner and started talking with a customer. As we got to know each other, he told me that Roger Staubach was one of his best friends. I mentioned to him that I just went to lunch with him the day before and was hoping to get to know him better. After our conversation, he offered to set up a lunch for the three of us. During lunch, I learned that the Staubach family plays flag football every year on Thanksgiving morning, and it was suggested that I should be his backup quarterback. Mr. Staubach agreed and allowed me to participate. I was over the moon to share the field with Roger Staubach. His family's tradition has now become my family's tradition by kicking off the Thanksgiving holiday with football. I've participated every year for the past ten years. We have visited each other many times now and are on a first-name basis, and even exchange Christmas cards. Roger Staubach is not just a mentor; he is a valued friend, and I am blessed to learn from him.

The values that make a great leader are very simple. Do what's right, aim to be respected, treat people well, and love your spouse. These are things that help you become a better person and a great leader.

Mr. Sewell has always been proud of my relationship with Mr. Staubach because I took his advice, shot for the stars, and created a friendship with such a great leader. He told me that he and Mr. Staubach were often at the same events in Dallas but didn't have anything in particular to talk about. Now that I've worked on this relationship, they have common ground to share.

THE VALUE OF MENTORSHIP

Mentors can provide insight and guidance because they have experienced more of life and can see the world from a different perspective. There have been countless times that a mentor has warned me that my actions could take me off track or have encouraged me to do something that could greatly benefit my circumstance. A good mentor does not allow fear to stop them from giving good advice. They understand risks versus rewards.

When my dad and I went to tour SMU, he could see far beyond what I could see. He knew that SMU was so much more than just a quarterback job. He saw the opportunity for a top-notch education, unbeatable connections in business or whatever I decided to pursue after school. As my dad, he knew how close I was to friends and family in Tehachapi. He knew that I was uncomfortable going to a college over fourteen hundred miles away from home. He did not let any hesitancy I might have stop him from telling me the truth and encouraging me to take advantage of the opportunity in front of me. Dad saw something positive before me and encouraged me to move toward it.

On the other hand, my middle school principal, Jim Hollen, saw me testing boundaries and experimenting with relationships that might lead me in the wrong direction. He encouraged me to move away from something potentially negative. He encouraged me to be more involved in my education, be a more well-rounded student athlete, and to stay the course. Without his guidance, my future could have been compromised.

As the mentee, being coachable is a key component of a successful mentoring relationship—especially when vying for a *shoot for the stars* mentor who may have limited time to devote to you. Be grateful for the time given and follow their direction and advice to help you grow. Even though the person may be an expert in their field and very accomplished, they need to feel valued as a person first and foremost.

LESSONS TO RISE ABOVE

Identify people to learn from. Who are your great teachers?
—Jacquelin Sewell
Co-President of Operations
Sewell Automotive Companies

Relationships create long-term success; honor them and invest appropriately.
—Joe Stallard
Chief Human Resources Officer
Sewell Automotive Companies

Be careful who you praise and admire. Be careful who you look down upon and wish to avoid becoming.
—Doug Thomas
American Professional Basketball Player

Humility is the pathway to knowledge.

—Fulton Sheen
American Bishop, Catholic Church

We all need heroes. Heroes remind us of what we can be, while inspiring us to grow.

—Jon Leonetti
Catholic Speaker, Author, Radio Host

EPILOGUE

As you can see from my story, I've had many challenges that didn't prevent me from aiming for the best in athletics, the classroom, at home, and in business. Success to me isn't about money or prestige but about leadership and stability. Although I didn't make it to the NFL, my current role in business is still feeding my competitive drive. I'm competing every day in a different way that allows me to continuously learn, grow, and evolve. Getting to this satisfying part of my career wouldn't have been possible without my mentors and coaches along the way.

I had people who believed in me and were always there to pick me up when I was down, love me, support me, and challenge me to rise above. I'm wired to strive for greatness and willing to do anything to push the boundaries. I've been blessed with great teachers and mentors who have poured into me and held me to a high standard to reach my full potential. Everybody needs someone to help them get from where they are in life to their next level.

OPEN DOORS

One of my key strengths throughout my youth has been overcoming adversity. Overcoming fear, anxiety, and adverse situations have made me into the person I am today. They say whatever doesn't kill you makes you stronger. In my experience that is true. I have overcome many struggles. Nothing was handed to me on a silver platter. To win the race, I had to seize the moment, make connections, and outwork my competition.

As a kid, I wanted to play professional sports. It was only when the journey ended, that I could mentally close that chapter that another door opened, and I could focus my energy on my profession and my family. The Sewell organization demands excellence, and this has been a catalyst for my growth and success into adulthood. Life will always hand you challenges that you must face and overcome. If you have faith in what you are trying to accomplish and faith in God, you can overcome fear. Faith is the opposite of fear and having faith will help you overcome any negativity that stands in your way.

CONQUERING FEARS

Throughout my youth there were instances that caused me great anxiety. I had no choice but to quit or rise above. My parents taught me how to face these fears directly. They did not allow me to avoid them.

Early on in my high school football career I feared failure. The varsity coach told the junior varsity coach that I was going to be one of the quarterbacks. I was the youngest player and had never taken a snap from the center in my life. I fumbled many times and was embarrassed in front of my teammates. If I didn't block out the noise and continue to practice, I never would have mastered the skills I needed to succeed.

In baseball in junior college, I had trouble with a specific drill, throwing the ball to home plate, or to the pitcher. With the spotlight on me, the pressure rose, and I failed over and over. I had to forge past my feelings and work hard to get it right and earn my spot on the team.

When I got to SMU, I fumbled in one specific drill all the time. Coach Bennett told me if I couldn't take the snaps properly, I would never play for SMU. I worried about this drill constantly. It was mentally overwhelming, but I had to move past my anxiety to practice over and over until it became second nature.

Later, I joined Sewell Automotive Companies and worked in the human resources department. Public speaking became a huge part of my career. While I was very good at it, I experienced a lot of anxiety and stress beforehand. Nobody could ever see it, but I could feel the worry and anxiety internally. It wasn't until about ten years into my career that I was finally comfortable with public speaking.

As I look back through the journey of my life, I realize that without overcoming each of these specific moments, I would not be where I am today.

The more you dominate your fears by facing and conquering them, the more value they bring to you. Addressing fear builds your confidence in your ability to win despite the difficult journey you may have to go through.

YOUR BEST LIFE

My hope is that my journey will inspire and motivate you to be the very best version of yourself. My victories came as a result of hard work, diligence, and belief in myself. Those around me have helped me look beyond the current circumstance and focus on the bigger, better vision of my future.

If you are struggling, find people who will support you, hold you accountable, and push you forward. Whatever you may face in life, you have the capacity to overcome it. Believe in yourself and find others who join you in that belief. No matter your age or circumstance, you have amazing capacity to do the work to achieve your dreams. Every challenge is an opportunity to grow.

Find purpose in everything you do, listen to those who have wisdom to offer, rise above, and you will live your best life!

LESSONS TO RISE ABOVE

My dark days made me strong. Or maybe I already was strong, and they made me prove it.

—Emery Lord
Writer

The older I get the less I listen to what they say. I watch what they do.

—Andrew Carnegie
American Industrialist and Philanthropist

The problem is not the problem. The problem is your attitude toward the problem.

—Jack Sparrow
Protagonist of the Pirates of the Caribbean

Whose prayer can you be the answer to today?

—Matthew Kelly
Motivational Speaker and Business Consultant

When you get to the top of the mountain, you become the mountain. Champions know they can get better.

—Nick Saban
Head Football Coach, University of Alabama

The secret in all victories lies in the non-obvious.

—Marcus Aurelius
Roman Emperor

ABOUT THE AUTHOR

Jerad Romo grew up in Tehachapi, California, and moved to Dallas in December of 2003 after being recruited to Southern Methodist University (SMU) for a football scholarship. He played quarterback for the Mustangs in 2004 and 2005. In 2006 he graduated with a Bachelor of Arts in Markets and Culture with a minor in Economics.

In 2007, Jerad joined Sewell Automotive Companies as a sales associate at Sewell Lexus Dallas. He has had the opportunity to work in many departments of the company: the recruiting department, in sales management at Sewell Lexus Dallas, and was the Director of Human Resources. He is currently the General Sales Manager of Sewell Lexus Dallas.

From 2012 to 2021, Jerad served as a mentor in Allies in Service, helping military personnel transition from service to the civilian world. He served as a member of the Undergraduate Industry Advisory Committee for Industrial Distribution and the Sales Leadership Institute's Advisory Board, both at Texas A&M University in College Station, Texas.

Jerad is currently on the board of Athletes United at Southern Methodist University, working to instill faith and fellowship in the current athletes on campus. He has also been a member of SMU's Lettermen's Board since

2006. This group works to connect current and former lettermen for the betterment of the university. He is a member of St. Monica Catholic Church in Dallas, Texas.

He enjoys spending time with his wife, Ashley, and his children, Katherine, James, and Allison.

Printed in the USA
CPSIA information can be obtained
at www.ICGtesting.com
LVHW090308230124
768656LV00035B/1191/J